# Libertine Literature in England 1660-1745

# Libertine Literature in England 1660-1745

## DAVID FOXON

*Thirteen Plates*

**UNIVERSITY BOOKS**  New Hyde Park, New York

# INTRODUCTION

I NEVER INTENDED to write a book about the origins of pornography, though it is a fashionable pursuit these days. By the time I had finished writing the articles reprinted here, I realized that a book was what I should have written; but equally by that time my thoughts had been expressed in one form and the impetus that might have made a book out of them was spent. Moreover, there were certain aspects of seventeenth-century thought which I would have had to explore deeply in order to round my work out, and I had already played truant long enough from my studies of eighteenth-century verse. What is printed here may, I hope, point the way for someone else to write that book; all I hope to provide is a sketch plan.

When I made the little find which started all this, I thought it would fill a couple of paragraphs in *The Book-Collector;* and as it grew with the help of John Hayward, its editor, these articles naturally found a place there. I say naturally, but the layman may wonder why it is natural for the book collector to be interested in dirty books. Certainly this is the case; Gustave Brunet (no relation to J. C. Brunet, the author of the *Manuel du libraire*) wrote many studies under his own name and under the pseudonym of *Philomneste junior* and was followed by other French scholars such as Paul Lacroix, Frédéric Lachèvre and Louis Perceau. This tradition of scholarly writing was never established in English, despite the work of H. S. Ashbee and Sir William Laird Clowes; but English and American collectors such as Richard Heber, George Daniel and Isaiah Thomas are early examples of the scholarly collector whose interest extended to pornography. In the nineteenth century these books figured in the sale catalogues of such continental collectors as Libri and Nodier, whereas in England and America their executors have concealed if not destroyed them; but the list of the distinguished collectors who are known is still a large one. What are the reasons for their pursuit?

Notoriously this class of literature appears in booksellers' catalogues under the heading 'curious', and nowadays it is almost alone under that heading. But fifty years or more ago that category included many other subjects which are now considered collectors' subjects in their own right — witchcraft and demonology, levitation and hauntings, frauds and fakes, together with early works on costume, early children's books, and accounts of technological experiments (particularly such failures as the search for perpetual motion). Until recently the book collector limited himself to a quite small range of intellectual subjects — literature and history, early printing and fine books — and books outside these spheres tended to be saleable only if they were in some way 'curious'; something, that is, which made a change from the everyday diet — as with such delicacies as caviar, piquancy was part of the attraction. Human beings tire of bread-and-butter, and also of the solemn; perhaps for this reason Romanesque churches have bizarre capitals to their pillars, renaissance decoration favors the grotesque, Leonardo was fascinated by caricature and book-collectors by the curious. Compare what Aretino says on p. 19 about erotic *jeux d'esprit*.

Another factor is rarity. Dirty books are inevitably among the rarest of rare books, having been produced surreptitiously, suppressed by authority, and destroyed by owners or executors; they only reach any standing in the serious book market centuries later. As a librarian, I have a dislike both of rarity and the collector's mystique that surrounds it. A librarian exists to make books available to others, and rarity continually stands in his way. In the first place it means that many works he feels are necessary to his collection are unavailable; or if they come on the market they do so at a price which he feels is not really commensurate with their scholarly value. Then, if the librarian has rare books in his charge there is the continual anxiety for them — not so much for the security problems which are comparatively obvious and can be satisfactorily met, but the problems of wear and tear. The British Museum suffers particularly in this respect, for even if there are ten copies of an important work in existence, probably half the scholars who wish to consult it will use the Museum copy, which means it gets ten times as much handling as the others. Requests for photographs or rapid copies mean exposure to a different set of hazards. The librarian is thus liable to irritation at the collectors' delight in rarity and is in danger of condemning them as on a par with those philatelists whose values are almost entirely those of rarity. Yet when I handle one of the two copies of the first, pirated, 1603 edition of *Hamlet*, I always do so with awe; and since writing these articles I have similarly had the privilege of handling two books discussed below which were believed to be lost. A copy of *Venus in the Cloister* 1725 (see p. 44) now belongs to Mr. R. Edgar Cox of Bournemouth and a xerographic copy is (thanks to his generosity) in the British Museum, while the Museum itself now possesses Cleland's own abridgement of *Fanny Hill* (p. 60). Having been so excited to see these rarities in spite of all my professional resistance, I can begin to understand what a powerful attraction rarity can have for the true collector. The best sort of book collector is aware of his role as the preserver of books and of knowledge which may easily be lost; these rare ugly ducklings whose survival is menaced by so many dangers therefore make a special claim on his attention.

Book collectors are also bibliographers, and to the bibliographer clandestine publishing is always a challenge. One thinks at once of the work of Professor Dover Wilson on the Marprelate tracts, those surreptitious Puritan pamphlets produced in the fifteen-eighties, the fascination of which led him into the revolution of Shakespearian editing which has been the centre piece of English bibliographical scholarship in this century. With such books the bibliographer is most of all the detective, seeking clues which will form a logical argument establishing the printer and date of a book, which will identify the earliest edition and possibly give a clue to the author or illustrator. For unlike the average book which has no need to conceal its origins, the author, printer and publisher of erotic works could be in considerable peril — indeed it is surprising to the outsider that they took such risks for such little profit. The first edition of Cleland's *Memoirs of a Woman of Pleasure* consisted of only 750 copies (Lewis Knapp in *The Library*, Sept. 1939) which sold for 6s., so the maximum profit can scarcely have reached a hundred pounds, of which Cleland is said to have received twenty. Yet all the participants spent an unpleasant time in gaol and under bond even though they seem to have been lucky enough to escape formal punishment. Others suffered more severely, as will be seen below.

As a result these books were always published anonymously or under a false name; the printer likewise concealed his identity and if possible the place of printing under a false imprint. Sometimes he merely put the name of another town, as the Paris printer of *L'École des filles* claimed it was printed at Leyden; at other times he chose a place like Villefranche or Fribourg or Freetown, which suggested liberty to publish. A step further is the invention of fictitious printers and places which Gustave Brunet studied in his *Imprimeurs imaginaires et libraires supposés*, 1866. Many of these, like 'chez l'imprimeur qui l'a imprimé, et en vente chez les libraires qui l'ont', or 'Printed at Helicon, beside Parnassus, and are to be sold in Caledonia' are quite entertaining; they are always confusing. Consider the imprint of the *School of Venus* given on p. 35: 'Rotterdam, printed by J. Johnson, 1,000,000'. The book was printed in London, not Rotterdam; Thomas Johnson had been a famous English printer at the Hague and Rotterdam some twenty years earlier; the date, of course, is meaningless. In some ways these obviously fictitious dates are the least misleading of all, for no one can take them seriously. More usually, these books give a correct date in their first edition, but after the authorities have suppressed them, subsequent publishers are likely to use the original date either in order to persuade the customer into thinking that he is getting a copy of the rare, suppressed first edition, or else in the hope that if the authorities take action against him, he can persuade them that he has not printed a new edition but is merely selling off a few copies left over from the first. So we have the situation explored in my appendix on the *Memoirs of a Woman of Pleasure* where there are at least four editions dated 1749 and the bibliographer has to decide which is the first — a task which in this case also involves discovering who the printer was. There

are a whole series of unsolved problems of this sort below — all
intellectual puzzles, made the more teasing by the difficulty of
finding the books which will provide the necessary clues. Difficulty is always a stimulus to the bibliographer; hence another
attraction for him.

We have still to consider the content of these books. To one
who like myself studied literature under C. S. Lewis with his
profound understanding of the way in which the unacknowl-
edged attitudes of different periods affected their literature,
there is always the hope that erotic writings may give some in-
sight into how people regarded a side of life which, though of
great importance to their life, is little discussed in their literature. To my mind the most important and unexpected discovery
in this study is the way in which pornography seems to have
been born and grown to maturity in a brief period in the middle
of the seventeenth century. I have only been able to make a
few tentative suggestions about the cause of this upsurge of
erotic writing; but it seems to me to show that however much
men remain the same in their erotic preoccupations, the form
in which these are expressed does vary, and that at this period
sex became to some extent intellectualized — a process which
may in some way parallel the poetic dissociation of sensibility
which T. S. Eliot noted in the same century.

At the same time this study does help to clarify the external
attitudes of society, as seen for example in the legal situation.
The position is not yet clear, but at least we now know that
there were prosecutions of obscene books forty years earlier than
the legal historians believed. Yet it seems clear that books like
*Venus in the Cloister* which were published without precipi-
tating legal action in the sixteen-eighties were liable to prosecution in the seventeen-twenties; similarly popular satirical works
like *The Fifteen Plagues of a Maidenhead*, which passed un-
noticed in the seventeenth century, suddenly attracted the
attention of the law in 1707. I think that here we can trace the
influence of the Societies for the Reformation of Manners, and
the increasing concern of the church with popular morality. It
is certainly clear that legal action against John Cleland was
largely inspired by Thomas Sherlock, the Bishop of London.

It is also clear that England was very closely involved in the outburst of libertinism on the continent. There is evidence that every time a major pornographic book appeared on the continent, it was known in England within the year, and in many cases appeared in translation right away. Moreover, we now know that of the six erotic works discussed here, at least four were reprinted in England in their original language. We have as yet no systematic study of the printing of works in foreign languages in England, but it is clear that the intelligentsia who were familiar with foreign languages provided a substantial enough market for *erotica*. In such ways there is a good deal of social interest to be learned from these books and their publication.

Of their psychological importance I am not qualified to write, though the publication of a chapter from Professor Steven Marcus's forthcoming book in the *Partisan Review* (Spring 1964) suggests that there is gold to be mined. The one thing that is obvious to the casual reader is the way in which what we have been educated to recognize as Freudian dream symbols are consciously and directly used by these writers as sexual metaphors. Many of these symbols, like that of the sword for the penis, can scarcely be called obscure; but the fact that they could be so freely used while to us they only appear in dreams suggests that our internal sexual censorship has become more severe with the passage of the centuries.

It would, of course, be vain to pretend that sexual curiosity is not as powerful a factor in the book-collector's interest in pornography as in the interest of the common man. Whether this fascination is merely a continuation of the child's curiosity about the sexual relationship of his parents, or a desire to learn new techniques, or to seek reassurance about his own capacities either on the level of reality or of fantasy, I have no idea; probably all these factors as well as others play their part in the furtive fascination that pornography holds. Perhaps this curiosity is a comparatively recent phenomenon as man has grown more civilized and more cut off from the directness of peasant life, and perhaps the seventeenth-century origins of pornography should be related also to this increasing civilization and the form it has taken in Europe. But it must be admitted that to some extent this general and furtive curiosity has tended to put all dirty books on the same level and to obscure their differences and their origins. Our increased psychological self-knowledge should help us to view the subject more rationally and to trace the beginnings and inter-relations of sexual writings more dispassionately, in the hope that thereby we can understand social and personal developments more clearly; and I would like to feel that this was an essay in that direction.

London, 1964.                                                    D.F.F.

# CONTENTS

# I

DURING A SEARCH for an anonymous poem I came upon the
following advertisement in the *Daily Advertiser* for Saturday 25
August 1744:

Because of the references to *L'École des Filles* in English literature,
and because no English translation was known to exist, this seemed
to deserve a short note. There followed a series of remarkable
happenings: every stone I disturbed revealed more wild life and
a whole series of discoveries forced themselves upon me. The
friends with whom I discussed the work were generous with facts
and theories, and I am deeply in their debt. It seems clear that most
amateurs of the subject have either had misguided ideas of what
research would be profitable, or a perhaps understandable dislike
of legal records. It would however be untrue to say that I have left
no stone unturned. This is primarily a rough account of what has
so far come to light about the publication of prose pornography in
England between 1660 and 1745. My attempt to define pornography will be found in the conclusion on p. 45.

¹ Holywell Street, famous for pornography in the 19th century, was opposite
St Clement's. [This note refers to the address in the line-block above.]

Recent authors have tended to assume that with the exception of Rochester's work there was no pornography in England in the 17th century and no successful legal proceedings against it until the action against Curll in 1727. On the contrary, it becomes clear that the English were very well aware of the outburst of erotic writing that took place on the Continent in the mid-17th century, were quick to import and naturalize it in England, and ran the risk of successful prosecution in doing so. With one late exception, however, all the books have disappeared. It has been a matter of surprise that of the less than twenty copies of Rochester's *Poems*, 1680 that survive, more than half represent different editions: editions multiplied, but copies vanished. But when one comes to the works discussed here, where it seems clear that editions likewise proliferated but that all trace of them is lost, Rochester's *Poems* are seen to be unique for their high survival rate which corresponds, perhaps, to their literary interest. The difficulties that face the bibliographer of erotica at the best of times can hardly be overstressed; I hope that these notes may show the possible importance of these English books and may be instrumental in bringing hidden copies to light.

Since the books discussed here are all translations or adaptations of foreign works, it seems necessary to give some account of their original publication and dissemination. Though some new information may be found here, together with an attempt to clarify the relationship between certain original works, much is highly derivative and is rarely based on a sight of the original editions—many of which appeared in the sale room a hundred years or so ago and have not been heard of since. If they could be traced, there would still remain much work to be done in determining their relationship and place of printing. As it is, I have used different authorities of varying trustworthiness with a cautious eclecticism.[2]

[2] 'Gay' =*Bibliographie des ouvrages relatifs à l'amour, aux femmes, au mariage . . . Par M. le C. d'I\*\*\** [i.e. Jules Gay]. *Quatrième édition . . . par J. Lemonnyer.* (Paris, 1894–1900). 'H/G' =*Bibliotheca Germanorum erotica & curiosa . . . Herausgegeben von Hugo Hayn und Alfred N. Gotendorf.* (München, 1912–29). 'Campbell' =a collection of bibliographical notes formed by J. C. Reddie who used the pseudonym of James Campbell: BM Add.MSS 38828-30. 'Brunet' and 'Graesse' are, I hope, self-explanatory. I have freely given locations in German libraries taken from the *Gesamtkatalog der Preussischen Bibliotheken*

The story for our purposes begins with Aretino. There are first of all the series of pictures of sexual activity designed by Giulio Romano for which Aretino wrote his *Sonetti lussuriosi*, and which eventually led to the genre of engravings known in England as 'Aretine's postures'; most references to Aretino in English literature from the 17th century onwards refer to these. Then there are his two series of *Ragionamenti*, printed in 1534 and 1536 and first collected in a London edition of 1584, which were widely disseminated throughout Europe and which, though not in themselves pornographic, were the model for all the subsequent works discussed here.

The earliest of these is the pseudo-Aretine *La Puttana errante*; next *L'École des Filles* of 1655, and then the 'classic' of French pornography, Nicolas Chorier's *Aloisiæ Sigeæ Toletanæ Satyra sotadica de arcanis Amoris et Veneris*, c. 1660. Finally some notes on *Vénus dans le cloître* are included because in English it became the subject of 'Curll's case' on which the English law of obscene libel was based.

This enquiry opens with a few references from English literature which may suggest that if these books had not been widely read by cultivated men, they were at least well enough known by name for reference to them to be quite comprehensible. These are followed by a chronological account of legal proceedings (there must be others I have not traced) to give some idea of the historical background. The rest of the article deals in some detail with the six major works, and ends with some general observations about their relationship to each other and to patterns of 17th-century thought.

### ENGLISH LITERARY REFERENCES

The earliest specific reference I know to a pornographic book is in Pepys's diary. On 13 January 1668 he 'stopped at Martin's,[3] my bookseller, where I saw the French book which I did think to have had for my wife to translate, called "L'escholle des filles", but when I come to look in it, it is the most bawdy, lewd book that ever I saw, rather worse than "Putana errante", so that I was

(vols. 1–14 only, Berlin 1931–39): there is no certainty that the books still remain there.

[3] John Martin, publisher to the Royal Society after the death of his partner, James Allestry, in 1670.

ashamed of reading in it'. However, on 8 February he was back at Martin's, 'and there staid an hour, and bought the idle, rogueish book, "L'escholle des filles"', which I have bought in plain binding, avoiding the buying of it better bound, because I resolve, as soon as I have read it, to burn it'. On the morning of the 9th he read a little: 'a mighty lewd book, but yet not amiss for a sober man once to read over to inform himself in the villainy of the world.' In the evening, after 'mighty good store of wine', 'I to my chamber, where I did read through "L'escholle des filles", a lewd book, but what do no wrong once to read for information sake ... And after I had done it I burned it, that it might not be among my books to my shame.'

Wycherley in *The Country-Wife* (I.i) makes Horner say: 'I have brought over [from France] not so much as a Bawdy Picture, new Postures, nor the second Part of the *Escole des Filles*.' Montague Summers in the Nonesuch *Wycherley*, 1924, quotes two further Restoration references, one of which, Learnerd's *The Rambling Justice*, 1678, similarly links *L'École des Filles* with 'Aretine's Postures'; the other, Ravenscroft's *The London Cuckolds*, 1682, complaining of the early maturity of girls, says 'the other day I catcht two young wenches, the eldest not above twelve, reading the beastly, bawdy translated book called the *Schoole of Women*'.[4] Tom Brown in his anonymous attack on Dryden, *The Reasons of Mr. Bays changing his religion*, 1688, criticizes his translating 'a certain luscious part of Lucretius ... [fit] only to keep company with Culpeppers Midwife, or the English translation of Aloysia Sigea'.

As for 'Aretine's Postures' themselves, they are closely linked with the history of scholarly printing in Oxford as is shown by the letter from Humphrey Prideaux to John Ellis of 24 January 1675 (ed. Maunde Thompson, Camden Society, 1875):

'The presse hath often furnished me with something to tell you. You little thinke it hath been imployed about printeing Aretins postures. I assure you we were like to have had an edition of them from thence were it not that last night the whole worke was mard. The gentlemen of All Souls had got them engraved and had imployed our presse to print them of. The time that was chosen for the worke was the eveneing after 4, Mr. Dean [Fell] after that time never useing to come to the theator; but last night, beeing imployed the other part of the day, he went not thither till the work was begun. How he took to

[4] Surely *L'Académie des Dames*: see Chorier's *Satyra sotadica*, p. 41 below.

6

find his press workeing at such an imployment I leave it to you to immagin. The prints and plates he hath seased, and threatens the owners of them with expulsion; and I thinke they would deserve it were they of any other colledge then All Souls, but there I will allow them to be vertuous that are bawdy only in pictures.' On 31 January he adds 'It was not all Aretine our gentlemen were printing here, but some of his more famous cuts for the private use of themselves and their friends. However, about 60 of them had gon abroad before the businesse was discovered; but Mr. Dean hath made them call them in again and commit them to the fire.'

### LEGAL PROCEEDINGS AGAINST OBSCENE BOOKS

The Licensing Act of 1662 was in force until the end of the Parliamentary session 27 May 1679, was revived from 24 June 1685, and expired again at the end of the session on 3 May 1695. It seems to have had little effect on what legal action was taken. The Committee of the Commons which considered the matter in 1695 felt that it was much more concerned to protect vested interests than the State and called it 'A Law which in no-wise answered the end for which it was made; the title and preamble of that Act being to prevent printing seditious and treasonable books, pamphlets, and papers: but there is no penalty for offenders therein; they being left to be punished at Common Law, as they may be without that Act'. (*Commons Journals* IX, p. 305.) There is in fact a general penalty in section 16: for the first offence any printer shall be disenabled from exercising his trade for three years, and for the second he shall be disenabled permanently and receive such further punishment as the courts may think fit; but the common law was certainly the chief weapon of the government.[5]

The main agents responsible for discovering and reporting unauthorized and undesirable printing were a group known variously as 'Messengers of the Press' or 'Messengers to the Press' who were directly responsible to one of the principal Secretaries of State;[6] their activities were authorized by the Act of 1662. Of these the most ubiquitous and unpopular was Robert Stephens,[7]

[5] For a recent study of methods of government control, see F. S. Siebert, *Freedom of the Press in England, 1476–1776* (Urbana, 1952).
[6] Siebert, *op. cit.* pp. 252–3; L. W. Hanson, *Government and the Press, 1695–1763* (London, 1936), pp. 29f.
[7] Leona Rostenberg, 'Robert Stephens, Messenger of the Press: an episode in 17th-century censorship', *PBSA*, XLIX (1955), pp. 131–152, and for the period

whose career can readily be traced in the indexes to the *Calendar of State Papers*. He had started informing by 1676, seems to have been a recognized agent by 1678, and was receiving government pay in 1680. Having turned Whig he was dismissed in December 1684, but returned at the Revolution.[8] The *Calendar of Treasury Books* shows him drawing a salary of £50 a year and £10 expenses up to 1718 (the latest volume published). The Stationers' Company made monetary gifts to him in 1679 and 1680 which became a salary of £10 a year between 1681 and 1684 and again between 1689 and 1697. They also paid him expenses for searches and legal fees.[9] Thus in the earlier period the messengers seem to have worked in collaboration with the Stationers' Company, but subsequently (when the Licensing Act was not in force) they were agents of the government alone. There are warrants for the payment of expenses of a Mr Kent recently deceased (12 March 1729) and to the new messenger Samuel Gray (21 March 1729) in PRO, SP44/83. The office was still in existence in 1770.[10]

The following list of government actions makes no attempt at completeness; it would, indeed, scarcely exist were it not for the kindness of Mr John Hayward. His researches into legal proceedings occasioned by Rochester's *Poems on several occasions* and by the play *Sodom* attributed to him turned up much of the information which I quote here. Prosecutions for obscenity, then as now, seem to come in clusters; I have omitted the proceedings against the Rochester editions except where they are directly linked to other books.

1660
J. B. Williams, *A History of English Journalism* (1908), p. 146,

after 1697 John Robert Moore, ' "Robin Hog" Stephens: Messenger of the Press', *PBSA*, L (1956), pp. 381–7.

[8] George Kitchin, *Sir Roger L'Estrange* (1913) pp. 327–8.

[9] See the receipts described by S. Hodgson, 'Papers and Documents recently found at Stationers' Hall', *Library* IV, 25 (1945), pp. 30–1.

[10] *The Trial of John Almon ... for selling Junius's Letter to the K—* (London, 1770) contains the following exchange on p. 49:
 '*Mr. Serjeant Glynn to William Bibbins*. You are a messenger to the press, please to tell us what that office is?
 *A.* It is my business to buy all political pamphlets.
 *Q.* Have you a salary for that purpose?
 *A.* There is a salary annexed to that office.'

records the imprisonment of John Garfield for writing the periodical *The Wandering Whore*, referring to S.P.Dom. 5 Oct. 1661: 'List of numerous prisoners now in Newgate, with the charges against them, and the dates of their committal.'[11]

## 1677

S.P.Dom. 3 Jan. 1677. Robert Scott to Sir Joseph Williamson:

'The bearer is Wells,[12] my brother-in-law, a bookseller, who, being lately set up in St. Paul's Churchyard, was so unhappy as to buy of Lucas,[13] a bookseller of Amsterdam, but then in London, several books, amongst which were some *Escole des filles*, *Aloyisiae Zigææ Amores* &c which he did not conceive in any way prohibited in England; but Mr. l'Estrange, having notice of it, sent his man to buy one, and next day, being yesterday, came himself and immediately caused his shop to be shut up several hours ... I humbly conceive this manner of proceeding of Mr L'Estrange was both illegal, unjustifiable and uncivil, for 'tis of ill consequence to cause a young man's shop to be shut up.'

## 1683

In S.P.Dom., 16 April 1683, Robert Stephens reports to Secretary Jenkins the offenders sentenced at the Guildhall Sessions: 'John Wickins for printing & publishing a book called *The Whore's Rhetorick* for which he was fined forty shillings'; Francis Smith junior for publishing a libel called *Matter of Fact* and *The Irregular Account of swearing the two pretended Sheriffs* was fined £10, Eleanor Smith daughter of old Francis Smith for *The Second Part of the Ignoramus Justices* was fined £10 and bailed for the second part of *The Growth of Popery*. Bills were found by the Grand Jury against James Ashwood for printing *The Packet of Advice* and against Joanna Broom for publishing *The Observator*.

This entry may serve as typical of the frequent occurrences of material about publishing in the State Papers; of the way in which prosecutions for political causes far outnumber prosecutions for obscenity; and the much larger penalties they then incurred.

[11] In *The sixth part of the Wandring-Whore revived* (London, printed for John Johnson, 1663. 4°: Bodleian) 'Eubulus' says 'I was committed to the Metropolitan Colledg of London [i.e. Newgate] upon a plea of trespass, for the non-payment of a hundred pound at the suit of one Gibson, where I continued 3 months before the publishing the fifth part of the Wandring-Whore.' The story needs further clarification.

[12] Probably George Wells.

[13] Possibly Jean Maximilian Lucas. See Kleerkooper & van Stockum, *De Boekhandel te Amsterdam* ('s-Gravenhage, 1914–16).

*La Retorica delle Puttane* was published in 1642; its author, Ferrante Pallavicino, was beheaded at Avignon two years later at the age of twenty-eight for his anti-clerical writings. In the form of a text book of rhetoric it describes a whore's life and the arts of persuasion she needs to learn; it is a satire not only on rhetoric, the Jesuits, and religion but also on sex and mankind. Like a Macchiavelli writing of private instead of public life he assumes that no emotion that is shown is real: all is a cover for some baser aim. It may be that by its attack on society as a hypocritical mask it made possible the pornographic works that followed;[14] but like the more genial satirist Aretino, Pallavicino uses sex as the material of his discourse: his aim is not to offer a sexual fantasy to the reader.

The English adaptation, *The Whores Rhetorick, calculated to the Meridian of London and conformed to the rules of art. In two dialogues,* has the [false?] imprint 'London, printed for George Shell in Stone-Cutter-Street in Shoe-Laine', 1683; there are copies in the BM and Bodleian.[15] It is odd, by the way, in view of the successful prosecution in April 1683, that it was advertised with this imprint in the *Term Catalogue* for Hilary 168$\frac{3}{4}$ (i.e. Feb. 1684) as 'The Whore's Rhetorick, or Mrs Creswel's last legacy'. (In the fourth edition of Clavel's *Catalogue*, 1696, it is listed with R. Downs as publisher.) This version follows the original quite closely at the beginning, but the bulk of the book has been turned into dialogue between Dorothea and Mother Creswel the bawd, bringing it into line with the form of the other works discussed here. Most of the rhetorical connotations vanish altogether, but it is enlarged with many contemporary London references, so that while the original direction of the book's satire has been lost, there is a new vitality in the whole.

1688

The Records of the Stationers' Company contain receipts for

[14] Cf. G. Spini, *Ricerca dei libertini* (Rome, 1950) for a study of Pallavicino in the wider context of the atheist, rationalist, and scientific anti-authoritarian tendencies of the 17th century.

[15] It was reprinted by James Maidment (Edinburgh, 1836) and by the Holland Press (London, 1960). Maidment attributed the translation to Sir Roger L'Estrange, but gave no authority for this rather unlikely attribution.

money paid to Henry Hills junior for buying books in 1688 and to Robert Stephens for legal expenses involved in prosecutions in 1689 and 1693. These were in their capacity as Messengers of the Press; although they were employed by the government, presumably the Company was paying expenses because it was their duty to prevent unlicensed publication. Hills's account (Plate I) shows that on 7, 8, and 9 March 1688 he had purchased copies of 'Rochesters Poems', 'The School of Venus', 'Tullia, Octavia', and 'A percel of Cutts' from booksellers all over London. Action had already been taken against the printers, for the City of London Record Office contains among the records of Guildhall Sessions the bonds given by Joseph Streater, Benjamin Crayle, and Francis Leach on 5 March.

Streater's bond reads 'for printing divers obscene & lascivious bookes, one called The School of Venus, another . . . a Dialogue between a Marridd Lady & a Maide';[16] Crayle's 'for selling several obscene and lascivious bookes'; Leach was responsible for Rochester's poems. The bonds were discharged at the Sessions on 23 April; Streater was fined 40s at Quarter Sessions 30 April 1688, and Crayle 20s at the General Sessions on 28 May; in both cases the indictment was for *The School of Venus* alone. The two were in trouble again in October 1689, Streater for printing and Crayle for publishing 'a play call'd Sodom or the Quintessence of Debauchery', sometimes ascribed to Rochester.[17] Stephens's account for obtaining these indictments is reproduced here (Plate II).

1696

*The Post Man, and the Historical Account* (Sat.–Tues., 10–13 Oct. 1696) has the following entry, which Mr Kenneth Monkman has kindly brought to my notice:

---

[16] The same as Hills's 'Tullia, Octavia'. See Chorier's *Satyra sotadica*, p. 41 below.

[17] No printed edition of *Sodom* survives: Heber is said to have had a copy which was destroyed by Dibdin after his death. Ashbee (II, p. 326) records an edition of 1684, probably on the authority of the Hamburg MS, which appears to copy a printed edition of that date. See J. Prinz, *John Wilmot* (Leipzig, 1927), pp. 390f. and p. 173 note 197. The fact that the edition proceeded against in 1707 ascribes it to 'the E. of R.' does little to help the controversy over its authorship.

'*London*, October 13. Yesterday about a Cart load of obscence [*sic*] Books and Cards, tending to promote Debauchery, were burnt near the Gatehouse at *Westminster*, by Mr. *Stephens* Messenger of the Press, in presence of a Justice of peace, and one Mr. Turner a Constable; they belong'd to one Bernardi an Italian.'

1707

So far the prosecutions I know of all took place at the sessions at the London Guildhall (I have not investigated the records of the Middlesex Guildhall which would presumably cover the 'West-End' retailers). The current batch of prosecutions were transferred from the Guildhall to the Court of Queen's Bench, where they were heard the following year, and the records are in the Public Record Office: (KB 28/21/18, 19 & KB 28/24/8, 9). It seems likely that the cases were transferred to the Queen's Bench because the government were anxious for more severe action than the small fines and recognizances imposed at the sessions. But though the juries brought in verdicts of guilty on the fact of publication in all the cases, legal argument in the first, Read's case, resulted in the indictment being quashed and the subsequent cases were adjourned *sine die*.[18] The decision in Read's case, reversed in Curll's case in 1727, seems to have turned on the point that there was no libel on any person but rather a general offence against morals: and this was a matter for the ecclesiastical courts. If the government were aiming at greater severity, the ground was cut from beneath their feet, and it is surprising that no pornographic efflorescence followed this legal incapacity.

James Read and Angell Carter were charged with publishing *The Fifteen Plagues of a Maidenhead*, one of a group of poems published in 1706 and 1707 with such titles as *The Fifteen Comforts of Matrimony*, *The Fifteen Comforts of Whoring*, *The Fifteen Comforts of a Wanton Wife*.[19] They are all half-sheet octavo pamphlets of near-chapbook style and very similar in typography to the cheap reprints published by Henry Hills between 1708 and 1710. The

[18] Rex *v* Read (1708) *Fortescue* 98.
[19] Observe the choice of a work for prosecution; sexual immorality in general may be written about, but virginity must be preserved. The titles probably refer back to *Les Quinze joies de mariage* ascribed to Antoine de la Sale; they may well all make mocking reference to such popular devotional exercises as *Les Quinze joyes de Nostre Dame*.

verse has much in common with the 17th-century ballads which could be bawdy without going any distance from the facts of everyday life. There are copies of the *Fifteen Plagues* in the BM and the Clark Library, Los Angeles (Plate III); and a reprint appeared in the Victorian period.

The two other cases in this year were against John Marshall for publishing *Sodom* and also 'an obscene play called The School of Love containing severall dialogues between Tullia and Octavia'. This is presumably another translation of Chorier's work.

1709

It seems worth recording here the trial of John Martin or Marten, surgeon, at the Queen's Bench (KB 28/31/20) because it is the earliest prosecution of an author in this series and because it concerns a medical manual on sexual relations. The indictment is that he 'being evil disposed and wickedly intending to corrupt the subjects of the Lady the Queene and seduced by cupidity, published and sold a scandalous book entitled Gonosologium novum, or a new system of all the secret infirmities and diseases natural accidental and venereal in men and women . . . written by way of appendix to the 6th edition of his book of the venereal diseases lately published and done with the same letter on the same paper, that those who please may bind it up with that.'[20] (Plate IV.) The BM copy is indeed bound up with the sixth edition of *A treatise of all the degrees and symptoms of the Venereal Disease* [1708]. The appendix is factual and practical, but it contains little that seems distinguishable in its culpability from the work it supplements; the whole work is heavily indebted to the earlier authorities J. B. Sinibaldus[21] and his popularizer Nicolas Venette.[22] Again, the indictment was dismissed.

[20] The indictment by the Grand Jury is referred to in *The Tatling Harlot* no. 2 26 Aug. 1709.

[21] *Geneanthropeiae* (Rome, 1642), an enormous folio from which selections were translated in 1658 as *Rare Verities, or the Cabinet of Venus unlocked* (BM, Glasgow University).

[22] *Tableau de l'amour consideré dans l'estat de mariage*, published anonymously and pseudonymously as by 'Salocini *Vénitien*' in several editions of 1687 and 1688, and subsequently as *De la génération, ou Tableau de l'amour conjugal*. Apparently first translated (from the eighth edition) as *The Mysteries of Conjugal Love revealed* in 1703 (*Term Catalogue*, Michaelmas 1703). There is a

1725–28

An account of the proceedings against Edmund Curll is given in Ralph Straus's *The Unspeakable Curll* (London, 1927) and a legal report in the *State Trials* (Cobbett's edition, vol. 17).[23] A translation by Robert Samber of Barrin's *Vénus dans le cloître* (for which see p. 43 below) was advertised on 15 October 1724 as *Venus in the Cloister: or, the Nun in her Smock*; a second edition was advertised on 4 February 1725. In the course of another drive against obscene books Curll was taken into custody for publishing this and Meibomius's *Treatise of Flogging* translated by George Sewell.[24] At the end of November 1725 he appeared at the King's Bench and was found guilty by the jury, but after some discussion of the legal difficulties caused by Read's case, 'it being a case of great consequence it was ordered to stand over for a further argument'. Curll emerged only to find himself back in custody at the beginning of 1726 as a result of further searches by the authorities, and as a result of his experiences in the King's Bench Prison he wrote *The Prisoner's Advocate*. In the King's Bench he also met John Ker of Kersland, the notorious government spy of Queen Anne's reign, and by publishing his memoirs he involved himself in a further charge at the beginning of 1727. In November that year he was still trying to evade sentence, and claiming in the *Weekly Journal* that *Venus in the Cloister* had been published by Henry Rhodes in 1683[25] without trouble. But no further argument was heard and Curll was finally sentenced in February 1728 to a fine of twenty-five marks for each of the two erotic works and a recognizance of £100 for a year's good behaviour; while for publishing Ker's memoirs he was fined twenty marks and ordered to stand in the pillory for one hour. The editor of the *State Trials* says of his appearance in the pillory, he 'was not pelted, or used ill;

copy of the third edition of 1712 in the Wellcome Medical Library; the BM copy was destroyed in the Blitz. This edition was used by Charles Carrington for his Paris reprint of 1906.

[23] There are a number of papers relating to the subject in the PRO, which Straus apparently used: see SP 35/55/102; SP 35/58/75, 99, 101; SP 35/61/9, 14, 30; SP 35/63/35, 36; SP 35/64/20–23 etc.

[24] The case argued in *State Trials* concerns *Venus in the Cloister* alone though Curll was sentenced on both charges.

[25] *Term Catalogue*, Easter 1683; apparently no copy survives of this or the Curll edition.

for being an artful, cunning (though wicked) fellow he had contrived to have printed papers all about Charing-Cross, telling the
people, he stood there for vindicating the memory of Queen
Anne'. It was in fact the case that Curll was in the pillory for the
political, not the moral offence; and the broadside he circulated
printed Queen Anne's warrant to Ker to stress this.

The judges in Curll's case seem to have accepted the argument
of the Attorney General:

'What I insist upon is, that this is an offence at common law, as it tends to
corrupt the morals of the king's subjects, and is against the peace of the king.
Peace includes good order and government, and that peace may be broken
in many instances without actual force. 1. If it be an act against the constitu-
tion or civil government. 2. If it be against religion. And, 3. If against
morality . . . 3. As to morality. Destroying the peace of the government;
for government is no more than public order which is morality. My lord
chief justice Holt used to say, Christianity is part of the law: and why not
morality too? I do not insist that every immoral act is indictable, such as
telling a lie, or the like: But if it is destructive of morality in general; if it does,
or may, affect all the king's subjects, it then is an offence of a public nature'.

1745

The drive against pornography in 1745 is documented by a
number of depositions, warrants, and minutes in the Public
Record Office (SP 36/65 and SP 44/83). On 19 March 1745,
E. Weston writes on behalf of the Secretary of State to John
Sharpe of the Attorney General's office, 'I send you inclosed by
Lord Harrington's order, two very obscene and infamous books
[marginal note adds 'Aretinus Redivivus & School of Venus'[26]]
which seem calculated for corrupting the youth of the nation; his
Lordship desires you will lay them before the Attorney General . . .
[for] his opinion how far the authors & publishers of them are
prosecutable.' On 27 March, Ryder, the Attorney General,
writes that the evidence against the persons is considerable; he will
know better after further examination of the witnesses what
chances there are of a verdict of guilty. Harrington formally
instructs the Attorney General to prosecute on 30 March.

A deposition by Edward Scudamore, a bricklayer of St
George's, Hanover Square, identifies copies of a collection of

[26] i.e. Chorier's *Satyra sotadica* and *L'École des Filles*.

engravings entitled 'A Compleat Set of Charts of the Coasts of Merryland wherein are exhibited all the Ports, Harbours, Creeks, Bays, Rocks, Settings, Bearings, Gulphs, Promontories, Limits, Boundaries &c';[27] he had bought copies at 5s a time from John Brett on 3 April and from Mary Torbuck on 5 April. Warrants were issued on 5 April for the authors, printers, and publishers of all three works.[28] A subsequent warrant dated 8 April recites that John Leake is printing off 'Venus in the Cloister or the Nun in her Smock in five dialogues adorn'd with Curious Copper Plates' and authorizes a search.

The depositions of the Brett family are very informative. John Brett says that the *Complete Set of Charts* sold on 3 April for 5s was fetched by his son from Thomas Read, price 3s 6d. *Aretinus Redivivus* had come from John Leake; Charles Brett adds that he had three copies from George Spavan at 5s a time and says, 'Spavan has long made it his business to sell all manner of bawdy books'. Copies of *The School of Venus* had come from Bridget, the wife of Daniel Lynch, a hawker; Catherine Brett adds that she also sent her sons to Mrs Spavan for it at 2s 6d a copy, and she has heard 'one Richards (first cousin to the said Spavan) say that Spavan had boasted of having got a guinea a week by the sale only of the School of Venus in particular'.

Of the wholesalers, Bridget Lynch 'own'd she had sold several

27 The work is not known to survive. The name of Merryland (clearly a pun on Maryland) must be related to the Ancient and most Puissant Order of the Beggar's Benison and Merryland, a phallic club started at Anstruther, Fife, in 1732 and formally inaugurated by a Code of Institutes signed on 14 September 1739. This and its offshoot the Wig Club—the wig (perhaps more accurately a merkin) was said to have been made from the pubic hair of Charles II's mistresses, and was added to by all new members—are described in Louis C. Jones *The Clubs of the Georgian Rakes* (New York, 1942); between them their members included George IV, four dukes, seventy-three peers and law lords of Scotland, thirty baronets and two bishops. The diploma of membership of the Beggar's Benison confers 'Our full powers and priviledges of Ingress, Egress, and Regress from and to, and to and from all the Harbours, Creeks, Havens and commodious Inlets upon the Coasts of Our said extensive Territories [i.e. of Merryland].' The Club Bible was offered for sale by Hugh Hopkins of Glasgow in his catalogue 98 (1962).

28 SP 44/83/460–1; also published in *Copies taken from the Records of the Court of King's Bench* (London, 1783), pp. 38, 39, a book of precedents compiled at the time of the proceedings against John Wilkes.

What Books bought since ye 6 March.
1688 By H: Hills Juni: in ye place of
messenger to ye Court.

|  |  | £ s d |
|---|---|---|
| March ye 7 | Wm Courton Powor Hill Rochestors Poems | 00:01:06 |
| 8 | The School of Venus | 00:02:06 |
|  | Hardings Man The Powd ally near Leatherfoilds | 00:03:06 |
| 8 | The School of Venus |  |
| 8 | Mr Tox Westminster Hall Rochester Poems | 00:01:06 |
| 8 | Willy – at ye Bible K's Street W: Ditto | 00:01:06 |
| 8 | Holford – at ye Crown Pall mall Ditto | 00:01:00 |
| 8 | Mr Lloyds Man West: Hall School of Venus | 00:06:00 |
| 9 | Mr Notts son Pall mall Tully & School Venus | 00:05:00 |
| 9 | Mr Canning in ye Temple School Venus | 00:04:00 |
| 9 | Mr Hardings man abinder. Ditto | 00:05:— |
| 9 | Mr Cownley at ye New Exchange Gallica Octavia | 00:02:— |
|  | a Widow near Mr Hardin of powd of bits | 00:09:6 |

Totall — 02:02:06

Brought over —— Totall — 01:07:06

£ – 03:10:0

March ye 10: 1688

Rec'd of Mr Christopher Wilkinson Warden £ 8–
in full of this Bill Three Pounds and Tenn
Shillings p me Hen: Hills Juni:

Rec'd for 3 dayes and a halfe for
Service for the Company of Stacioners
attending the messinger. Eight shillings
and nine pence p me Charls Church

PLATE I. HENRY HILLS'S SHOPPING-LIST
The account rendered by Hills to the Stationers' Company for buying copies of
suspect books in March 1688. 248 × 195 mm
(Stationers' Company Records, by permission of the Master and Court)

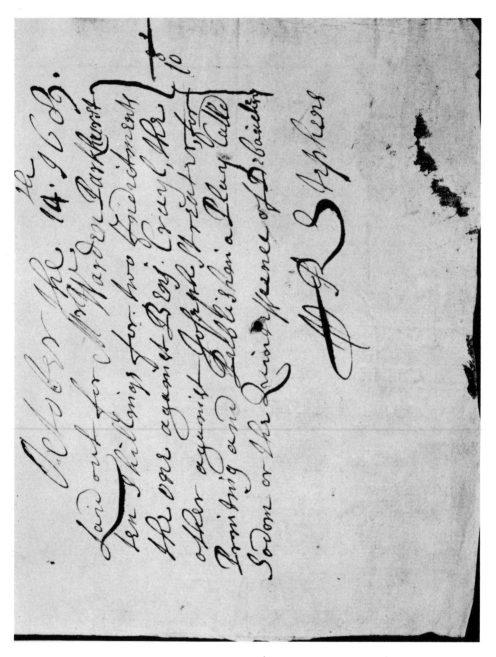

PLATE II. EXPENSE ACCOUNT OF A 'MESSENGER TO THE PRESS'
Robert Stephens's statement of expenses for indictments against Benjamin
Crayle and Joseph Streater for 'Printing and Publishing a Play Calld Sodom
or the Quintessence of Debauchery'. 140 × 178 mm
(Stationers' Company Records, by permission of the Master and Court)

# THE
# Fifteen PLAGUES
## OF A
# Maiden-Head.

Written by Madam *B-----le*.

### LONDON:
Printed by *F. P.* near *Fleet-street,* 1707.

PLATE III. THE SUBJECT OF 'READ'S CASE'
Note the unauthorized use of the arms of Cambridge University. 174 × 109 mm
(British Museum)

published but by himself. He was not concerned in the *School of Venus* or *Aretinus Redivivus*. He surrendered forty-seven *Charts of Merryland* and the plates. He also surrendered all the sheets of 'The History of Don B.'[32] and all the cuts belonging to it, and promised never to be concerned in printing, engraving or publishing the like again.

[32] Hayn/Gotendorf (Bd. 3, 1913, p. 581) records a copy of *The History of Don B    . Translated from the French*. 1743. 8° at the Staatsbibliothek Hamburg, but this was destroyed in the last war. It was a translation of *Histoire de Dom B*★★★★★, *portier des Chartreux* by J. C. Gervaise de Latouche. What is apparently the first edition ('à Rome, chez Philotanus', pp. 318, copy at the Bibliothèque Nationale) is usually dated as *c*. 1745; it is clearly earlier. It was illustrated, according to Hayn, with 26 plates, according to Gay with 23; the plates are said to have been engraved by Caylus. An unillustrated and undated edition with the same imprint but 209 pages is in the BM; from the ornaments and press figures it was clearly printed in London *c*. 1745.

# II

THE STORY OF these pictures is told by Vasari thus: 'Giulio Romano caused Marcantonio to engrave twenty plates showing all the various ways, attitudes and positions in which licentious men have intercourse with women; and, what was worse, for each plate, Messer Pietro Aretino wrote a most indecent sonnet . . . Since some of these prints were found in places where they were least expected, not only were they prohibited, but Marcantonio was taken and thrown into prison.' It seems clear that the original designs were by Giulio Romano, that Marcantonio Raimondi engraved sixteen plates in 1524, that Aretino, inspired by the plates, wrote the sonnets to accompany them about 1525, and that these were in print by 9 November 1527 when Aretino sent a copy to Cesare Fregoso. There seem to have been early copies of the plates and the set was extended to twenty early enough for Vasari to accept that number as correct.

Aretino's dedication to Battista Zatti of Brescia, reprinted in his *Lettere* of 1538 from the *Sonetti sui 'Sedici modi . . .' di Giulio Romano*, is worth translating *in extenso* as a clue to Aretino's views:

> After I had persuaded Pope Clement to release Marcantonio Bolognese who was in prison for having engraved the *Sedici modi*, I felt a desire to see the pictures which set off Giberti's complaints that this brilliant artist ought to be crucified; and when I had seen them I felt the same spirit which moved Giulio Romano to draw them. And since poets and sculptors both ancient and modern have from time to time written or carved erotic things as *jeux d'esprit* (such as the marble satyr in the Palazzo Chigi which is trying to violate a boy), I rattled off the sonnets which you see at the foot of each page. Their wanton memory I dedicate to you (*pace* all hypocrites), for I renounce the bad judgment and dirty habit which forbid the eyes to see what pleases them most. What harm is there in seeing a man on top of a woman? Must animals have more freedom than we? It seems to me that the you-know-

what given us by nature for the preservation of the species should be worn as a pendant round our necks or as a badge in our caps, since it is the spring that pours out the flood of humanity and the ambrosia drunk by the world on its great festivals. It has created you, one of the first living surgeons; it has made me, who am better than bread. It has brought forth the Bembos, the Molzis, the Fortunis, the Franchis, the Varchis, the Ugolin Martinis, the Lorenzo Lenzis, the Dolcis, the Fra Bastianis, the Sansovinis, the Titians, the Michelangelos; and after them the popes, the emperors and the kings; it has produced the pretty children and the beautiful women with their *sancta sanctorum*: and for this reason we should decree holy days and dedicate vigils and feasts in its honour, and not hide it away in a scrap of cloth or silk. The hands would be well hidden, for they gamble, make false oaths, lend at usury, make rude gestures at you, tear, pull, punch, wound and kill. And what of the mouth that swears, spits in the face, devours, makes you drunk and vomits? In fact our legislators might gain some respect if they would only put a footnote in its favour in their loathsome books; perhaps they will. Meanwhile, see if in my verses I have drawn the attitudes of my players to the life. If you are writing to our friend Frasino, send him my good wishes.

Clearly there is some special pleading here, but the Renaissance spirit of free exploration is also present. It is not without significance that Titian was re-creating the sensual female nude in the 1520s, and that Marcantonio above all others was making known the nudes both of classical antiquity and of his contemporaries.

As one might expect, research and curiosity are both bedevilled by the failure of prints to survive. The last recorded set and its fate is described in *Nollekens and his Times* by J. T. Smith, first published in 1829:[1]

> Mr. Nollekens was in possession of a set of those extremely rare engravings, from the Aretin subjects, so often mentioned by print-collectors: but it so happened, as he was glancing at them one day, that his Confessor came in, who insisted upon their being put into the fire, before he would give him absolution. I once saw them; and he lent them to Cosway, to make tracings from them. However, this loan Cosway stoutly denied, which when Nollekens heard, he exclaimed, 'He's a d—d Liar! that every body knows; and I know this, that I could hardly get them back again out of his hands.' Upon Nollekens being asked how he, as an artist, could make up his mind to burn them, he answered, 'The priest made me do it': and he was now and then seen to shed tears for what he called his folly. He was frequently questioned thus: 'Where did you get them, Sir? whose were they?' His answer was, 'I brought them all the way from Rome'.

A print of the first engraving of the series is in the British

[1] London, 1920 edition, vol. 1, p. 295. 'Antiquities' Smith was subsequently Keeper of Prints and Drawings at the British Museum.

Museum Print Room:[2] its survival may be explained since the position conceals the sexual organs. It differs from the copy described by Bartsch (vol. 14 no. 231)[3] in not bearing the number '1', and since the engraving is rather coarse it may well be from an early copy of Marcantonio's plate. The Albertina is reported to have an engraving of no. 11 which is said to be of similar quality; the fragment of this composition in the BM is from a different and better plate. This is one of nine innocuous fragments (Plate VI), which are referred to in a letter of Pierre Mariette dated May 1756.[4] Though they are not listed separately in his sale catalogue, Ralph Willett bought Mariette's Marcantonio prints *en bloc* and the fragments can be traced from his sale through the collections of Sir Mark Sykes and Sir Thomas Lawrence to the British Museum. I can find no trace of other surviving copies.

A related book is described by Mr Walter Toscanini in 'Le operette erotiche aretinesche' in *Il Vasari*, anno 19 (1961) fasc. 1.[5] This is a 16th-century edition of the *Sonetti* with woodcut illustrations, wanting A1 and A4; the former was the title and the latter bore the fifth and sixth sonnets. The woodcuts are reversed, but otherwise correspond exactly with the plate and fragments in the BM. The borders of several cuts are broken and the text has many errors, which leads me to suspect that the edition is neither authorized nor very near in date to 1525. It is of prime importance, however, as the only recorded edition of the original text and illustrations to survive.

The situation is complicated by the activities of Count Frédéric de Waldeck,[6] who issued in 1858 a lithographed text as an intro-

---

[2] I am deeply indebted to Mr John Gere of this department for many of the facts relating to these prints; the interpretation of the facts is, of course, my own responsibility.

[3] In the De Fries collection, not the Albertina as Delaborde (see below) assumed; lot 122 in his sale at Amsterdam, 21 June 1824. A copy (possibly the same one) was in the Wellesley collection (Sotheby, 29 June 1858, lot 402) together with a copy of no. 2 (ditto, lot 403).

[4] In Christoph Gottlieb von Murr, *Journal zur Kunstgeschichte* vol. 14 (1787) pp. 22, 23.

[5] It previously belonged to Max Sander who discussed it in detail in *Zeitschrift für Bücherfreunde*, N.F. XXI (1929) pp. 50–60.

[6] Jean Frédéric Maximilien comte de Waldeck died at the age of 109 in May 1875. For his life see *Thieme-Becker* and refs. and also Mary R. Darley Smith, *Recollections of two distinguished persons* (Philadelphia, 1878).

duction to a series of facsimiles of the twenty prints which he claimed to have found and copied in a convent when he was in Mexico City in 1831.[7] It seems likely that the price he asked ('le prix de chacun les met . . . hors du domaine publique') was too high to make it worth while to engrave them, for both the BM and Bibliothèque Nationale have the illustrations in pen-and-wash.[8] It is clear that in comparison with the genuine fragments the figures are much weakened and the backgrounds modified and given additional furnishings in a neo-classic style after the manner of Prud'hon. To further confuse matters, his numeration in no way corresponds to what seems the original order. But in ten of the fourteen cases where Waldeck can be compared with the wood-cuts in Mr Toscanini's volume, the positions of the figures agree exactly. In three others there are no similarities at all, and the final case exposes Waldeck's claim to reliability, for Waldeck's plate 12 agrees with Toscanini's woodcut no. 9 only in so far as they are linked by a fragment in the BM: that is to say, the BM fragment showing the upper half of a woman's body corresponds exactly to the woodcut, while Waldeck has improvised an entirely different scene around the genuine fragment. It seems almost certain that apart from the BM fragments Waldeck must have had access to at least ten genuine prints or tracings of them which he then had to eke out with his own pastiches to complete the set of twenty; if he had limited himself to the original number of sixteen, his task would have been lighter.[9] As to the source of his materials, it seems probable that while the Mexican convent is invented, there is some truth in the account he gives of the discovery of eleven prints by F. A. Gérard about 1808; Gérard is said

[7] Henri Delaborde, *Marc-Antoine Raimondi* (Paris, [1888]) pp. 238–47, has a full and scholarly study of the engravings and a critical account of Waldeck's efforts, but is not entirely reliable. It is from him I take the date and the authorship of Waldeck's prospectus. Frederick Hartt's *Giulio Romano* (New Haven, 1958) quotes Waldeck (with some errors) *in extenso*, but subjects him to no critical tests.

[8] Delaborde speaks of sets of photographs of the drawings as the normal method of publication: he may be right, in which case these two sets are special copies. They are remarkable works for a man in his nineties.

[9] In his plate no. 10 Waldeck has made a free copy of an engraving of Leda and the swan (of which the BM possesses a state signed by Agostino Veneziano, *Bartsch*, XIV, no. 232) to pad out the set.

to have made tracings before selling them via Samuel Woodburn to an English duke, and some time after Gérard's death in 1843 Waldeck succeeded in getting hold of these tracings. Eleven tracings would certainly give an almost perfect explanation of the partial accuracy of his reproductions.

Subsequent developments are shrouded in mystery.[10] It seems likely from references to twenty plates and sonnets that the original series was extended. By the late 17th and early 18th century sets of twenty-four and thirty-six[11] erotic plates are regularly referred to and associated with Aretino's name, but they have no relation to the original series. What seems to have happened is that *La Puttana Errante* was published over Aretino's name about 1650; it describes and then tabulates thirty-five postures. With a frontispiece this would have called for thirty-six plates, and I suspect that whatever its origins the text in this form may have been produced to accompany illustrations: Romeyn de Hooghe was charged with having engraved plates for a new edition in 1677. That the sonnets were forgotten and 'Aretine's postures' associated with the dialogue can be seen in Chorier's

[10] Christoph Gottlieb von Murr, *Journal zur Kunstgeschichte* vol. 14 (1787) pp. 1–72 contains a very full and learned account of many materials not now to be found. It describes in particular sixteen plates engraved in Holland from drawings by Annibale and Agostino Carracci at the end of the 16th century, but from the descriptions they seem to have no relation to the sonnets. *L'Arétin d'Augustin Carrache* [Paris, 1798], a quarto with twenty plates and a text attributed to S. C. Croze-Magnan, shows in some plates an indebtedness to the original Giulio Romano designs.

[11] There is no completely satisfactory explanation for the numbers involved: Giulio Romano's original sixteen and the twenty-four and thirty-six of the 17th and 18th centuries. It is tempting to associate them with the fact that the normal small format of the books they illustrated changed from 8° to 12° between these times. R. H. van Gulik, *Erotic Colour Prints of the Ming Period* (Tokyo, 1951) relates that the albums of erotic prints which were produced in China between 1570 and 1640 most commonly showed twenty-four postures; twenty, thirty, and thirty-six are also found. It is by no means impossible that such albums could have found their way to Europe, but the number of the months makes multiples of twelve good round figures in East or West. According to the proceedings against Mathijs van Mordechai Cohen in 1768 (*Kleerkooper & van Stockum*, p. 31) 'het boekje genaamt "L'École des filles", bekent is onder de naam van "Chineesche Almanach"'. Cohen used the same set of prints to illustrate *L'Académie des Dames* and *L'Histoire de Dom B✱✱✱* as well as *L'École des filles*.

*Satyra sotadica* of 1660, at the end of the sixth dialogue: 'Aevo nostro, divini vir ingenii, Petrus Aretinus, bene multas [posturas] in colloquiis suis expressit satyrico sale: post, pictura, Titianus et Carraccius, summi pictores.' The French translation of 1680 makes the identification with *La Puttana Errante* clear: 'Pierre Arétin . . . en a exposé trente-cinq dans ces colloques, que Titian et Carrache . . . ont ensuite dépeintes et tirées d'après nature'. The earliest set of these plates I have seen (quite well designed, but crudely engraved) illustrates an 18th-century edition of *La Puttana Errante* ('Venetia', *c.* 1720, belonging to Mr J. I. Davis) which is illustrated with a frontispiece and thirty-five plates; the same subjects, reworked and in new settings, are used to illustrate a French translation of Chorier, *L'Académie des Dames* ('A Venise chez Pierre Arretin', *c.* 1775). The plates have some relevance to the former work, but none to the latter; and they are quite different from the original Giulio Romano subjects.[12] It seems fair to say that there may have been a number of new sets of plates designed 'after the manner of Aretine' in the 17th and 18th centuries; but that they are likely to have been copied and used as illustrations with little if any thought of their relevance to the text they accompany.

In England there is little that is certain before the prosecutions of 1745 when there were four illustrated books and a set of plates involved.[13] There is the reference to the printing of Aretine's postures at the Oxford Press in 1675, the 'percel of Cutts' bought by Hills in 1688, and a prosecution against Matthew Heatley, Hans Mullins, and Peter Bouch for publishing indecent pictures

---

[12] It is, perhaps, worth noting as an aid to identification that the original series contains one cut of a couple making love on a cart drawn by Cupid. The *Puttana Errante* set contains a cut with a woman in a basket, here matching the text; but no doubt because of the exotic nature of the position it is usually set in a tropical background with a coloured couple. This posture was mentioned in a humorous context by Aretino in the first day of the *Ragionamenti* (1534); it seems to have captured the popular imagination. A bas-relief version closely following the design of the plate in Mr Davis's *Puttana Errante* is among the five erotic tiles found recently in one of the upper rooms of The Cheshire Cheese in Fleet Street: they are probably English workmanship of about 1750 and are on deposit at the Guildhall Museum.

[13] Illustrated editions of *The School of Venus* (24 plates), *Aretinus Redivivus* (24 plates), *Venus in the Cloister*, and *The History of Don B✶✶✶*; and the *Charts of Merryland*.

(KB 28/24/11, 12) in 1707. The most illuminating reference is an interpolation in the English adaptation of Pallavicino, *The Whore's Rhetorick*, 1683. Where Pallavicino recommends 'Le figure dell'Aretino' the English reads:

> Mother *Creswel*. *Aretin*'s Figures have no place in my Rhetorick, and I hope will find no room in my Pupil's apartment. They are calculated for a hot Region a little on this side *Sodom*, and are not necessary to be seen in any Northern Clime.
>
> *Dorothea*. What do you mean by *Aretin*'s Figures?
>
> M.C. Only, Child, Six and Thirty Geometrical Schemes which he drew for his own diversion.
>
> *Dor*. What have I to do with those hard names, are those tame things to be had here?
>
> M.C. Four and Twenty rough draughts may be had for money.
>
> *Dor*. Pray tell me of something I understand, and which is proper for this cooler Region. Though I have an itch to know what you mean by the Figures, for I am sure it is something else than what you have yet told me.
>
> M.C. *Aretin*, Daughter, among other things was a great Astronomer, and particularly had an exquisite knowledge in the nature of *Mars* and *Venus*, and in all the Seasons, and varieties of their conjunction.

## ARETINO: *RAGIONAMENTI*

Little need be said here of the *Ragionamenti* of Aretino; texts are readily available, a critical edition is in preparation by Professor Giovanni Aquilecchia,[14] and there is a considerable critical literature. They provide a realistic and satirical view of the lives of women in different occupations; their main importance here is that the form they take—a dialogue between an older and a younger woman—is one which remained the norm for at least 150 years: it is followed in all the works discussed here.

The main series consists of two sets of three dialogues published in 1534 and 1536 respectively;[15] they were collected in a series of editions (which added some apocryphal pieces) with the imprint of 'Bengodi, 1584'. For details of these I am indebted to the un-

---

[14] 'Per l'edizione critica delle sei giornate di Pietro Aretino', *Italian Studies*, XVII (1962) pp. 12–34.

[15] The *Ragionamento de le Corti* of 1538 and the *Dialogo . . . del gioco* of 1542 are unrelated except in form, though they were published as *La terza et ultima parte* in the London edition of 1589 (*STC* 19913).

published researches of Mr Denis Woodfield.[16] The first was printed in London—outside the range of the *Index Expurgatorius*, but largely for the continental market—by John Wolfe between October 1584 and January 1585 (pp. 219; 373; 116: BM C.107.aa. 32 & Clare, Cambridge). The title of the BM copy (Plate V) has the signature 'W. Cecill' on the title: presumably it is the copy sold with Lord Burleigh's books by Bentley & Walford, 21 Nov. 1687 ('libri italici' lot 263, sold with 262 for 1s 2d—a comparatively high price). The second edition was printed by John Windet for Wolfe about 1597 (pp. 228; 401; 142: BM 1079.c.5, Bodleian, Clare, etc). Four later editions were printed on the Continent: [Amsterdam, *c.* 1600] (pp. 198; 339; 118: Bodleian 8° A.97 Art); [Amsterdam, *c.* 1620] (pp. '698'; 339: BM 12470.aa.25); [place and date unidentified] (pp. 522: BM 245.e.20); and one with a chronogram at the end of parts 1 and 2 'MeDICata reLabor' [1649 or 1651] (pp. 198; 339; 118: Bodleian Vet.B.3 f.292).

The third day of the first part of the *Ragionamenti* which deals with the life of whores in a dialogue which discusses their lives realistically but not obscenely had a very wide circulation by itself in many languages and must accordingly have had a good deal of influence. It seems first to have appeared in the same year as the complete edition of part 1: *Opera noua del diuo & vnico signor Pietro Aretino: la qual scuopre le astutie, scelerita, frode, tradimenti . . . che vsano le Cortigiane* (Neapoli, 10 Nov. 1534: BM; Venetia, 15 Jan. 1535: BM; Neapoli, 1547: Staatsbibliothek Berlin). It was translated into Spanish by F. Xuarez as *Coloquio de las damas* (Seville, 1547: Staatsbibliothek Munich; Caragoça, 1548: Munich; [Seville?] 1548: BM; Medina del Campo, 1549: Bibliothèque Nationale; [Seville?] 1607: BM, Bodleian). From Spanish it was translated into Latin by Caspar Barthius as *Pornodidascalus, seu colloquium muliebre* (Francofurti, 1623: BM, Bodleian; Cygneae, 1660: Bodleian, Bibliothèque Nationale).[17] It was also translated from Spanish into German as *Italiänischer Huren-Spiegel . . . Aus der hispanischen Sprach . . . übergesetzt und zum ersten Mal in Truck verfertigt* ([*c.* 1655]: Staatsbibliothek Berlin; Nürnberg, 1672:

---

[16] See also Harry Sellers, 'Italian books printed in England before 1640', *The Library*, ser. 4, vol. 5 (1924) pp. 114–16.

[17] This must not be confused with Barthius's translation of the Spanish novel *Celestina*, published under the title *Pornoboscodidascalus* at Frankfurt in 1624.

Mazzuchelli.)[18] In Dutch it appeared as *Het leven en d'arglistige treken der courtisanen te Romen* (Leyden, [1680]: Royal Library, The Hague, Halle University).

A number of French works are listed as translations, but I cannot confirm them all: *Le miroir des courtisans* (Lyon, 1580: BM); *Tromperies dont vsent les mieux affetées courtisanes* (Paris, 1580: *Brunet*); *Histoire des amours faintes et dissimulées de Lais et Lamia* (Paris, 1595: Bibliothèque Nationale; Lyon, 1599: *Graesse*; Paris, 1602: *Graesse*); *Dialogue de l'Arétin, où sont desduites les vies et déportements de Lais et Lamia* ([Paris, 1611?]: *Brunet, Graesse*; reprinted 1871: BM); *Dialogue de l'Arétin, où les vies, & faits de Lais, & Lamia courtisanes de Rome sont déduites* ([no imprint] pp. 96: Bodleian; [no imprint] pp. '202' for 102: Staatsbibliothek Munich).[19] A free adaptation in English is *The Crafty Whore: or, the mistery and iniquity of bawdy houses* (Henry Marsh: London, 1658: BM, *Wing* C6780).

## LA PUTTANA ERRANTE

*La Puttana Errante, overo dialogo di Madalena è Giulia* claims to be by Aretino and follows the same dialogue form as the *Ragionamenti* in which the elder woman takes the greater share: but it is almost entirely devoted to Madalena's sexual autobiography as a thread on which to hang most of the possible positions for sexual intercourse. It is the first imaginative prose work which deals directly and exclusively with physical sexual satisfaction, though this is garnished rather sparsely with some moments of emotion and glimpses of ordinary life. It ends with a named catalogue of thirty-five postures, which explains why sets of plates became associated with it; it might originally have been written as an explanatory text to pictures, but its origins are obscure.

[18] *La Vita di Pietro Aretino*, 1763. Graesse records an edition of 1602, presumably in error for 1672. This title has previously been listed as a translation of *La Puttana Errante*, but the reference to the Spanish confirms the present attribution by the *Gesamtkatalog der Preussischen Bibliotheken*.

[19] A[dolf]. G[erber]., *Kurze Uebersicht über die mir bekannten reichlich 200 Aretino-Ausgaben und Uebersetzungen des 16. und 17. Jahrhunderts* (1923) lists other early French editions, but in so abbreviated a form that I have not been able to incorporate them here.

Modern authorities all agree that it is not by Aretino,[20] and the first edition under this title seems to be an undated Elzevir edition, printed to accompany a new edition of the *Ragionamenti* in 1660. The appearance in London of John Garfield's periodical *The Wandering Whore* at the end of 1660 tends to confirm that date, for evidence over the next hundred years shows a very brief time lag between a Continental publication and its English repercussion. Garfield's work had no connection with the text of *La Puttana Errante*; he was clearly cashing-in on a new and notorious title.

Yet the title itself does not belong to this prose work; it originally belonged to a verse satire by Lorenzo Veniero, a disciple of Aretino who wrote it not earlier than 1538.[21] It has been suggested by Alcide Bonneau[22] that the Elzevirs applied the title to a reworking of the first part of *Dialoghi doi di Ginevra, e Rosana. Composto da M. Pietro Aretino detto il diuino* (Stampata nella nobil città di Bengodi, 1584). This work of 124 pages seems to have been printed to accompany the last collected edition of the *Ragionamenti* listed above which has the chronogram date of 1649 or 1651.[23] Unfortunately I have been unable to trace a copy: that listed in the *Catalogue des livres imprimés de la Bibliothèque du Roy* (*Belles Lettres*, tom.2. (1750) p. 71: 'Ouvrages licencieux') was lost from the Bibliothèque Nationale before the creation of the 'Enfer' about 1880.[24] We therefore have to rely on the testimony of M. Hubaud who reported that the first of these two dialogues in which Rosana tells her story was very similar to *La Puttana Errante*, though the names of the characters have been changed. We do not know what was in the second dialogue which

---

[20] It is ascribed to Niccolò Franco, Aretino's secretary, by Mr G. Legman in his introduction to the New York reprint of Ashbee's bibliography (1962); but he gives no authority for the attribution. Since Franco imitated all his master's manners, he is a possible candidate.

[21] It has been erroneously dated 1531 and ascribed to Aretino himself: this is clearly wrong. cf. L.-J. Hubaud, *Dissertation littéraire et bibliographique sur deux petits poèmes* (Marseille, 1854) who gives the fullest account of the problem known to me.

[22] *Curiosa* (Paris, 1887) pp. 250 ff.

[23] Hubaud *loc. cit.*

[24] I am indebted to Mme Veyrin-Forrer, Conservateur à la Réserve, for her help here. The Floncel catalogue (Paris, 1774; no. 4708) records a manuscript version, not a printed text.

contained Ginevra's story; but it is interesting that Giulia says at the beginning of *La Puttana Errante*: 'Tu dirai quelli che hai provati . . . e se per caso io n'havero provato alcuno piu di te lo diro, talche tuttili trovaremo.' This certainly opens the way to a second dialogue, and its irrelevant presence in *La Puttana Errante* suggests incomplete revision. The dates of recorded editions also suggest the priority of the *Dialoghi doi*, but since Hubaud thought he detected two hands in the two dialogues and thus tended to the view that the second was a later addition to *La Puttana errante*, the question must remain an open one. It seems advisable for the present to accept a date of *c.* 1650 for the first known printed version as *Dialoghi doi*. The authorship remains a mystery.[25]

Willems in *Les Elzevier* (Bruxelles, 1880; no. 858) discusses the two editions of *La Puttana Errante* without imprint published to accompany their editions of the *Ragionamenti*; he gives priority to that with 54 pages (BM) as 1660 and dates that with 38 pages (BM, Bodleian) as 1668. The Bodleian has a small octavo of 59 pages (Linc. 8° F.9: Barlow's copy, so earlier than his death in 1691) which looks early and uses lower case 'v' and 'u' according as they occur initially or medially, unlike the Elzevirs which follow modern usage. It shares all the obvious misprints I have noted which are common to the two Elzevir editions; it also has one or two variants of its own. In one case it uses an initial capital 'V' (in 'Vndecimo') agreeing with the 54-page Elzevir as against the 38-page. There is a 48-page edition of the early 18th century with the false imprint 'Venetia' in the private collection of Mr Davis, and a 62-page edition with press figures (BM, V & A—

---

[25] It has been suggested that *La Puttana Errante* was based on the *Dialogo de la bella creanza de le donne* by Alessandro Piccolomini, probably first published in 1540. Such an idea can rest only on determined ignorance, since there are a number of modern editions readily available (e.g. in *Trattati del cinquecento sulla donna, a cura di Giuseppe Zonta* (Bari, 1913) in the series *Scrittori d'Italia*). The dialogue is indeed in the usual Aretinesque form and starts with advice about dress, the care of the body, conduct in society, the choice of a lover; and at the very end the *ingénue* is offered a specific lover for whose benefit the dialogue has been arranged. The dialogue is concerned with the destruction of innocence, the need for hypocrisy, and the importance of gathering rosebuds at the proper time; but there is no obscenity and the whole is based on the concepts of ideal love and nobility of spirit. The suggestion that adultery can be a proper fulfilment of love is, of course, part of one tradition of courtly love.

Dyce) which is clearly 18th-century English. Gay records an 84-page edition which I have not traced.

The earliest translation appears to be Dutch, entitled *De dwalende Hoer*, which was banned in 1669; the famous engraver Romeyn de Hooghe is said to have engraved plates for a new edition in 1677.[26] The first separate French translation seems to be *La Putain errante* (Lampsaque, 1760: BM); a later edition as *Vie de l'Arretin ou entretiens de Magdelon et de Julie* (1783: BM); it did, however, appear together with *L'École des filles* in *La Bibliothèque d'Arétin* ('Cologne', *c.* 1690: Bodleian), a collection subsequently reprinted under the title *Cabinet d'Amour et de Vénus* ('Cologne', *c.* 1690: Gay; 'Au Mont Parnasse', 1693: Gay). The first German translation is *Gespräch zwischen Magdalena und Julia* (1772: H/G). All the authorities list as an English translation *The Wandering Whore* of 1660, but this is a completely different work, a periodical with various continuations.[27] In fact the earliest English translation seems to be *The Accomplished Whore. Translated from the Puttana Errante of Pietro Aretino. By Mary Wilson, Spinster* (London: printed for the translator, 1827; in fact published by George Cannon; see Ashbee, *Index librorum prohibitorum*, p. 1).

L'ÉCOLE DES FILLES

*L'École des filles* keeps the Aretinesque form of a dialogue between an experienced woman and a virgin, but adds a simple plot. Robinet has fallen in love with the young Fanchon who is too innocent to know what his tentative approaches to her mean. Robinet becomes the lover of Susanne her kinswoman, and then persuades her to speak for him to Fanchon. In the first dialogue Susanne explains the pleasures of love and the foolishness of chastity and encourages Fanchon to try the adventure with Robinet; he enters as Susanne leaves at the end of the first dialogue. In the second dialogue a week or two later Fanchon tells Susanne

---

[26] W. P. C. Knuttel *Verboden boeken* ('s-Gravenhage, 1914) p. 57; Thieme u. Becker Bd. 17, p. 460 and refs.

[27] Parts 2–4 of *The Wandering Whore* (Dec. 5–19) are in BM. *The fifth and last part* (1661) and *The Sixth part of the Wandring Whore revived. Written by Peter Aretine* (London, printed for John Johnson, 1663) are in the Bodleian. There is also *The Wandring Whore's complaint for want of trading* (London, printed for J. Jones, 1663: Bodleian) and *The Wandering Whore, a Dice Rogue* (1663: Hazlitt, *Handbook*, p. 655).

of the pleasures she has had and asks many questions for a fuller understanding of her experiences.

Although the work is clearly immoral or obscene in so far as it attacks social conventions, it has certain endearing features: it is concerned with the genuine pleasures and excitements of physical love rather than the contrived and intellectualized lusts and perversions, and it has a mixture of downright commonsense and psychological perception which makes possible some worthwhile observations on sexual relations. Take, for example, the sensible tone of the following exchange from the English translation of 1744, called forth by Katy's graphic description of a memorable night of love:

> *Fanny:* Is it possible such excessive lewdness could please you?
> *Katy:* Why not? When one loves one another these things are very pleasant and serve to pass away the time with a great deal of delight . . .

*L'École des filles* was first published in 1655, a fact known for many years only from a letter of Guy Patin dated 17 August 1655:[28] 'On a ici pendu en éffigie un nommé Milot, avéré autheur d'un infâme livre intitulé *L'Eschole des Filles*, que l'on dit estre tiré de l'Arétin.' However, Frédéric Lachèvre ran to earth the dossier of the trial in the Archives Nationales and published an admirable account of the whole episode in his *Mélanges* (Paris, 1920). The documents are also reprinted as an appendix to the new edition of the work edited by Pascal Pia (Paris, 1959). Although they give a great deal of information about the production of the book, the problems of authorship are not finally solved.

Two men, Michel Millot and Jean L'Ange, ordered 300 copies of the book, fifty on fine paper, to be printed by Louis Piot. Millot bore three-quarters of the cost and L'Ange the remaining quarter. The printing was completed in May 1655 without a licence and with the false imprint 'A Leyden'; the partners took delivery of all the sheets. L'Ange took some copies to the binder, Louis Framery, who bound twenty-two in parchment under close supervision; eight of these (presumably fine paper presentation copies) went to the poet Scarron. At this stage the printer and binder, having been paid for their work and well aware of the danger of their position, thought it prudent to inform the

[28] Wrongly dated by earlier authorities as 26 July.

authorities through Robert Ballard, *syndic des libraires*, in return for a guarantee of their immunity. On 12 June, L'Ange had an appointment with Nicolas de la Vigne, a bookseller who was going to buy fifty copies. The authorities were aware of this, and waited for him to keep the appointment, arrested him and searched his apartment, seizing his remaining copies and a manuscript of the work in his hand containing passages omitted in the printed text. They also seized copies at Millot's apartment, but though they saw Millot it did not for some reason seem prudent to arrest him.

L'Ange, then, was alone in custody. At his first examination he made a gallant attempt at bluff, suggesting that the author might have been the comte d'Etelan or the comte de Cramail; that he was given the books in payment of a debt by a M. Dumas; that they had been printed at Leyden. On 13 June, confronted with the detailed evidence that the authorities had, and knowing that Millot had escaped, he admitted that the manuscript was in his handwriting, but said the work was composed by Millot; all he had done was to help with the editing and cutting certain parts 'parce qu'ils l'ont cru trop libre'; he had also corrected the proofs. In his final interrogation on 4 August, he modified his statement slightly by saying that Millot was 'l'autheur ou traducteur'. The final judgment was that L'Ange was banished from Paris for three years, fined 200 *livres* and ordered to make formal penance, while Millot was sentenced to be hung (in effigy, since he had escaped arrest) and burnt with the books, and all his property was forfeit. Sentence was passed on 7 August, carried out on 9 August, and on 11 August Millot made a formal appeal against sentence, claiming that he had been on duty with the army in Lombardy all the while these slanders had been put about. The appeal was accepted and there is no trace of further action against him. There is a suggestion that he probably never left the neighbourhood of Paris and the proceedings against him were something of a sham.

Two alternative hypotheses concerning the authorship then present themselves. If Millot was safely out of the way, and perhaps under the protection of someone important, L'Ange might safely put the blame on him even if he wrote it himself. On the other hand Millot might have been protected as a cover for some more illustrious author. Pierre Loüys, fascinated by the

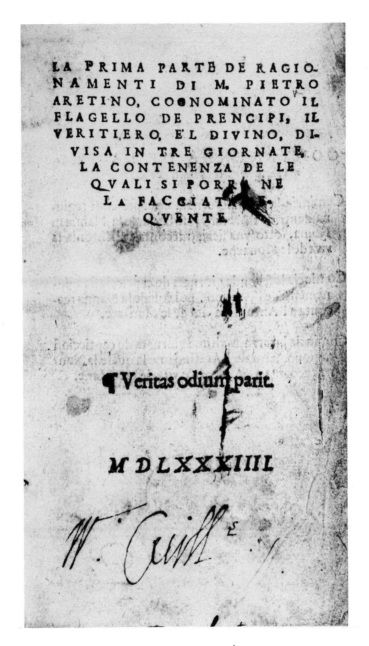

LA PRIMA PARTE DE RAGIO-
NAMENTI DI M. PIETRO
ARETINO, COGNOMINATO IL
FLAGELLO DE PRENCIPI, IL
VERITIERO, EL DIVINO, DI-
VISA IN TRE GIORNATE,
LA CONTENENZA DE LE
QVALI SI PORRA NE
LA FACCIAT
QVENTE

¶ Veritas odium parit.

MDLXXXIIII

PLATE V. LORD BURLEIGH'S COPY
The first collected edition of Aretino's *Ragionamenti*, printed in London by
John Wolfe, 1584. *STC* 19912. 163 × 94 mm
(British Museum)

7(w3)

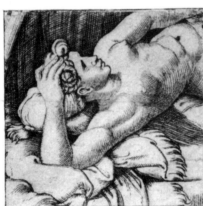

*left and above* 5 or 6 (w4)

2 (w15)

PLATE VI. MARIETTE'S FRAGMENTS OF GIULIO ROMANO'S *SEDICI MODI*
The fragments are engraved by various hands. The numeration follows Mr
Toscanini's edition; Waldeck's numbers (pencilled on the original mount) are
supplied in parentheses. According to Waldeck, fragments 5 or 6, 2, 9 are by
Marcantonio; 4, 7, 10 by Cavaglio; 11 by Marco Dente. The fragments are
on a mount 215×245 mm; they are rearranged here and reproduced in the
original size. Some have been extended in pen-and-ink to fill their frames
(British Museum, Dept. of Prints & Drawings)

10 (W19)

11 (W2)

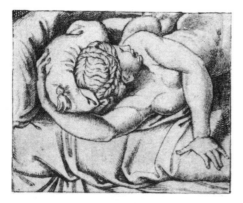

9 (W12)

4 (W11)

4 (W11)

PLATE VII

# L'ECOLE

## DES

## FILLES

M. DC. LVIII.

---

*Left:* THE GENUINE WORK

The earliest edition of which a copy has been traced. Probably printed in Holland. 131×76 mm (British Museum)

*Right:* THE PIOUS FRAUD

The only known copy of an imitation earlier than any surviving edition. 129×76 mm (Bayerische Staatsbibl. Munich)

---

# L'ESCOLE

### Des

## FILLES,

### où

## LA PHILOSOPHIE

### Des

# DAMES.

Divisée en

## DEUX DIALOGUES,

Agere & Pati.

*Corrigé & augmenté, d'un combat du . . & du . . . d'une Dialogue enre le . . . & Perrette; & une instruction des Curiositéz, dont la methode de trouver, est marqué par leur nombres suivant les tables.*

Imprimé a Fribourg;
chez ROGER BON TEMPS;
l'An. 1668.

fact that the only copies known to have been circulated were the eight that went to Scarron, suggested that the author might be Scarron's wife, the future Madame de Maintenon! Or, more seriously, could it be Scarron himself? The *Gazette burlesque* which he had edited from the beginning of the year suspended publication for the month of July, and No. 17 for 4 August has some verses from his successor as editor wondering what had become of him, just as if he had disappeared.[29] The gap covers the period of the legal proceedings when Scarron would have been well advised to keep out of the way if he were the author. The powerful protector might have been the Surintendant des Finances, Nicolas Fouquet, the amoralist to whom Scarron dedicated *Le Gardien de soi-même* which was published that same July. Certainly after Fouquet's sensational fall from favour in 1661, the inventory of a house furnished by him for one of his mistresses records a copy of the 'Leyden' edition which the searchers burnt.

That is the last recorded trace of the first edition, but Dutch reprints followed soon. Those recorded are 'Paris', 1659 (*Gay*); 'Paris', 1667 (*Lachèvre*); 'Fribourg', 1668 (BM) (Plate VII); 'Paris', 1671[30] (*Graesse*); 'Fribourg', 1676 (*Campbell*); 'Ville Franche', 1686 (*Gay*); and an early undated edition of Liège (*Gay*).[31] Jacob Benjamin of Amsterdam printed two Dutch editions, one of 1658 and one undated; the title was *L'École des filles of de schoole voor de jonge dochters, door D.v.W.* (Kleerkooper & van Stockum, p. 3). The earliest edition of the German translation, *Die Jungfern-Schule*, 'Paris' [i.e. Frankfurt], is variously given as 1733 (*Gay*) and 1737 (*H/G*).

One pitfall dug for the student is worthy of note. The *L'École*

---

[29] *Scarron et sa Gazette burlesque*, edited by F. Lachèvre, Paris, 1929.

[30] A 1672 Paris edition is also recorded; it may be merely a variant imprint, or else the work described in the following paragraph.

[31] The title says 'enrichi de trente-sept belles figures en taille-douce', but the plates do not survive. The Regent, le duc d'Orléans, is said to have had twenty-four plates engraved to illustrate the book, from which forty copies were printed (von Murr, *Journal zur Kunstgeschichte*, vol. 14 (1787) p. 48): these too are lost. *Hayn/Gotendorf* records a copy of the 1671 edition with plates—presumably the illustrated edition referred to in a document of 31 Aug. 1671 quoted by E. F. Kossmann, *De Boekverkoopers, notarissen, en cramers op het Binnenhof*, ('s-Gravenhage, 1932), p. 33.

*des filles* of 1658 (Plate VII) at the Bayerischer Staatsbibliothek, Munich (A-B¹², A-E¹²) is not the earliest surviving edition but a pious fraud which may well be related to the *L'Escole des filles, en dialogues* (Paris and Avignon, 1672) recorded in Barbier, *Diction- naire des ouvrages anonymes*, vol. 2, col. 18. An 'Epistre aux filles' signed R. D. V. tells the girls in the best libertine tradition that they need not be afraid of the book calling a spade a spade, and that they are made for love and delight. There is then a brief first part of twenty-four pages, at first divided as lessons in dialogue form between mother and daughter, about love, beauty, youth, physical pleasure, and how to deceive a jealous husband: the temperature rises quite high and the language gets direct. But then follows the second part 'où sont contenus les vrays et solides enseignemens d'une fille', which starts by decrying the loose talk and morals that are so prevalent, saying 'si . . . ie vous ay depeint les fausses apparences de l'Amour: c'estoit pour vous laisser un dégoût & une aversion dans vostre Ame'. There follow 120 pages of cures for evil thoughts and wrong behaviour—prayers, the Virgin, the mass. It is a surprising piece of propaganda.

Copies of the original work in French had reached England by January 1668, when Pepys bought his copy. The first trace of an English edition to be found is the prosecution of Streater and Crayle for printing and publishing *The School of Venus or the Ladies delight reduced into rules of practice*,[32] in 1688. Only a brief extract is quoted in the indictment, but it is enough to establish that it is in fact a translation of *L'École des Filles*. Susanne and Fanchon have become Frank (the elder girl) and Katy, while the lover Robinet becomes Roger.

The next recorded appearance is in 1744, a prelude to the prose- cutions of Lynch and Stevens in 1745. Here we have the help of newspaper advertisements, one of which started the present investigation and is therefore reproduced on page 3; but with- out the books it is not always easy to interpret advertisement evidence. The earliest reference seems to be in the *Daily Advertiser* for 24 July 1744:

[32] Not to be confused with *The School of Venus; or Cupid restor'd to sight . . .* *By Capt. Alexander Smith* (Morphew, 1715) nor Curll's *The School of Venus: or, the lady's miscellany* (second edition, 1739)—though they may have been intended to be confused with it.

Sold by Jacob R binſon, at the Golden Lion in Ludgate-Street.

*This Day is publiſh'd, Price (only) 1 s.*
Adorn'd with a curious Copper-Plate Frontiſpiece,

THE School of Venus, or the Lady s Deli ht, reduced Into Rules of Pr. & ce. Tranſlated from the French *L'Eſcoles des Filles.* In two Dialogues between Frances, a married Lady, and Kitty, a young Maiden.

*Dicite Grammatici cur Maſcula Nomina Cunnus,*
*Et cur Fœmiriam Mentula Nomen habet.*

Sold at the Pamphletſhops over-againſt St. Clement's Church in the Strand, and at the Royal Exchange.

*This Day is publiſh'd ( Price ... )*

About a month later there are a series of advertisements, in the *General Advertiser* 20 August, the *Daily Post* 21 August, and the *Daily Advertiser* 22 August, similar to that reproduced on p. 3. Though the wording varies, the common factors are an edition at 3s 6d, illustrated with twenty-four curious copper plates, and sold by John Stevens and the pamphlet-shops. In the *London Evening-Post* for 21–23 August comes a reply from the first publisher:

*Juſt publiſh'd, Price* 3 s. 3 d.

THE School of VENUS, &c Adorn'd with 24 curious Plates, &c.

N. B. As there is juſt publiſh'd a pirated Edition of this Book, printed on a ſmall Letter, with the Cuts done in a very wretched Manner, Price 3 s. 6 d. therefore Gentlemen may know the true Edition by this Token (*Rotterdam, printed by* J. Johnson 1,000,000)

To be had at the Places before advertiſ'd, Price 3 s. 3 d. the Proprietor being reſolv'd always to ſell his Book for 3 d. leſs than the pirated ſort, tho' this is 1 s. better.

Alſo to be had at the ſame Place only,

The original French, with 36 curious Plates, Price One Guinea.

It is this which caused Stevens to warn the public against 'those innumerable blunders which are to be found in every page of the Irish edition, merrily call'd a Dutch one, and sold by the Irish hawkers' in the *Daily Advertiser* and *Evening-Post* between 25 and 30 August.

It thus appears that there was first an 'Irish' edition with a frontispiece at 1*s*; that Stevens later published an illustrated edition at 3*s* 6*d*; and that his rival hastily added plates to his edition, raising his price to 3*s* 3*d* while still undercutting Stevens. But what is meant by the description of this as an Irish edition sold by Irish hawkers? Without a copy of the 'Rotterdam' edition we cannot determine whether it was indeed printed in Ireland; but we have a possible clue in the reference in the depositions to Bridget, 'the wife of one Lynch, a hawker'. Lynch was subsequently convicted of publishing *The School of Venus*, and as a hawker with an Irish name it seems likely that he had a close connection with the earlier edition and was the object of Stevens's attack.

No copy of either edition survives, but the judgments of the Court of King's Bench against Lynch and Stevens[33] contain a transcript of most of the text, though not, unfortunately, the passage quoted in the 1688 indictment; we cannot therefore tell if the same translation was being used. Unfortunately, too, both judgments seem to quote from the same edition, so that we cannot confirm that Lynch and Stevens had published independent texts. It may be that in 1688 and 1744 there are three independent translations, or merely editions of the same one. The text which does survive is a fairly free[34] but lively translation and abridges the original somewhat, especially the more metaphysical passages; the girls are now called Fanny and Katy; Fanny's lover in the French has become her husband in English. The advertisement referred to twenty-four plates, which form part of the indictment; the first few are referred to by numbers in the text. Presumably they were bound together at the end, and hence the addition made to the French original on p. 22:[35]

*Katy.* . . . It seems this pleasure has many postures.

*Fanny.* Yes above a hundred, have you but a little patience and I will describe them by the help of a little book I have here which will show you every different posture as I go on in my description.

---

[33] KB 28/176/19, 20.

[34] One interpolation in Fanny's advice deserves notice:' . . . and by thy private f———ing thou wilt attain to a kind of confidence which is much wanting to most of our English ladies.'

[35] The judgment has marginal references to the pages of the printed edition throughout: it seems to have had about eighty pages.

'J. Campbell'[36] in the late 19th century recorded *The School of Venus, or amorous fancies and the postures of love described in two instructive and confidential dialogues between a woman and a virgin. Translated from the Italian of Pietro Aretino* (no imprint, 70 pp. 12°), and noted that it was not from Aretino but from *L'École des Filles*.[37] This also seems to be lost; it was almost certainly produced after 1750.

[36] BM Add. MS 38829 ff. 381, 382.
[37] He also suggested that it might be the same work as the *Dialogue between a woman and a virgin* (Printed for R. Borewell, South Audley St, 1786: 35 pp. 12°) which was reprinted in *The Voluptuarian Cabinet* of 1824. These also seem to have disappeared, but Ashbee's description (*Catena* p. 315) shows that it is not immediately related: if anything it descends from Chorier's work.

# III

THE DIALOGUES BY Nicolas Chorier seem to be the third of this group of erotic classics; they are certainly the most advanced pornographically. They are still in dialogue form, but the women engage in erotic action together as well as discussing it, and they are later joined by male actors. The plot continually provides new shocks as apparently stable background figures like mothers and husbands are disclosed as having highly irregular relationships; it is as though a series of gauzes were lifted showing each time more complex groupings. As a demonstration of the falsity of appearances and the hypocrisy of society it is brilliantly anarchistic. There is a strong sadistic flavour in parts of the work, with much stress on defloration. Stylistically and technically it may well deserve the praise which French scholars have bestowed on it; but it may equally seem repugnant.

The original Latin edition of Nicolas Chorier's work, which purports to be a translation by the Dutch scholar Meursius of a Spanish work by Luisa Sigea of Toledo, appeared as *Aloisiae Sigeae Toletanae Satyra Sotadica de arcanis Amoris et Veneris. Aloisia hispanice scripsit, latinitate donavit Ioannes Meursius* about the year 1660. Isidore Liseux[1] dates what appears to be the first edition as 1659 or 1660, and instances the absence of catchwords as showing it to be a piece of French printing; comparing it with Chorier's earlier work printed at Lyons, he suggests it was printed there. Edmond Maignien in *L'imprimerie . . . à Grenoble* (Grenoble, 1884) suggests that it was printed at Grenoble by Pierre Frémon for Jean Nicolas: both names vanish from Grenoble imprints between 1660 and 1668 as though they were under an interdict. Chorier himself moved to Grenoble at this time. There was only

---

[1] 'La première édition des dialogues de Luisa Sigea' in *La curiosité littéraire et bibliographique*, sér. 2 (1881).

one dated edition out of some 15 before Barbou's edition of 1747, so there is plenty of work for bibliographers.[2] The first edition can be recognized by six pages of errata at the end of the first part (pp. 245;111: Techener and Libri sales; a copy was catalogued by Asher of Berlin at £1 in 1865); there follow two related editions (pp. 165;78: *Liseux*; pp. 171;81: *Graesse*, supplément). Subsequent editions are enlarged: 'accessit colloquium ante hac non editum Fescennini ex MS. recens reperto'. There is a dated edition of 1678[3] (Amstelodami, pp. 1–224; 225–324;161: BM, V & A-Dyce) and three undated editions (pp. 177;98;155: BM; pp. 217;306: sold at auction by Beijers, Utrecht, 17 May 1949, lot 67; pp. 166;238: BM). An edition with a new title which was universally adopted in the 18th century, *Johannis Meursii elegantiae Latini sermonis* (BM), has the same collation as the last of the previous group and would, if the sequence were neat and logical, mark the end of phase one. Probably the descent of the text is far less straightforward than that.

The first French translation was apparently made by Jean Nicolas, *avocat* of Grenoble and son of Jean Nicolas the *libraire* associated with the first Latin edition.[4] The BM apparently has the only known copy of the first edition: *L'Académie des dames, divisée en sept entretiens satiriques* (A Ville-Franche, chez Michel Blanchet, 1680: Plate VIII). It is in two parts (pp. 295;112), the second containing the seventh dialogue; it has also an errata leaf to testify to its priority. The remarkable thing about this edition is that 'Campbell' reports it to be the only one with the complete text; subsequent editions not only omit passages throughout, but also cut the final dialogue by a half. The Nodier catalogue of 1844 (no. 983) records *Les sept entretiens d'Aloisia* (Cologne, Ignace-le-Bas, 1681); Brunet and Graesse do not agree on its collation, but both come very close to that of the BM copy, and since it also had an errata leaf it may well have been another issue of the 'Ville-

---

[2] One reason for the number of surviving editions is doubtless the decent obscurity of the Latin language which saved it from the fate of its vernacular cousins. Copies still turn up in the antiquarian book trade in this country; my own was printed in England, for it contains a tailpiece cut by Francis Hoffman and probably dates from the 1730s.

[3] There is a tradition that the enlarged edition was first printed for Chorier in Geneva; but I have not been convinced of its validity.

[4] Cf. *Barbier* under *Académie des Dames.*

Franche' edition. According to the bibliographies, subsequent editions proliferate under various titles, but the only one I can verify is *L'Académie des dames ou les sept entretiens d'Aloysia*. One group has a Cologne imprint,[5] the other 'Venise, chez Pierre Aretin'.[6]

A new translation appeared as *Nouvelle traduction de Meursius, connu sous le nom d'Aloisia ou l'académie des dames. Revue, corrigée et augmentée* (Cythère, 1749) but subsequent editions sometimes applied this title to the old translation.

The earliest trace of the work in England is a manuscript translation, dated 1676, of Book IV ('The Duell'), which forms part of a commonplace book at Princeton (MS AM 14401, pp. 137–234). The early printed translations and adaptations are again known from prosecutions: *A Dialogue between a married lady and a maid* in 1688, *The School of Love* in 1707, and *Aretinus Redivivus* in 1745. There is, however, a curious prologue. In 1681 there appeared *Aloisia, or the amours of Octavia Englished, to which is adjoyned the history of Madam du Tillait, both displaying the subtilties of the fair sex* (London, printed for Jacob Tonson, 1681: Newberry Library, Chicago). This is undoubtedly a sucker-trap, for though it is a translation of 'Alosie. Ou les amours de Madame de M.T.P.' from *Amours des dames illustres de nostre siècle*,[7] the names of the charac-

---

[5] A 1691 edition of 324 pages at the Bibliothèque Nationale and Munich, and an undated edition at Munich. Graesse records Cologne editions of 1688, 1693, 1700, and 1730 under the title *Aloysia ou l'Académie des dames*; Gay records the same dates with the title *Aloysia ou entretiens académiques des dames*.

[6] An undated edition of 310 pages in BM and an undated edition at Munich. 'Gordon de Percel' [i.e. Nicolas Lenglet du Fresnoy] in *De l'usage des romans* (Amsterdam, 1734) records an edition of 372 pages and another 'la plus belle, on la distingue en ce qu'au lieu de chiffre en haut de la page il y a un petit fleuron. J'en ai vu où il y avait des figures au nombre de trente-six, qui sont un peu sales pour les imaginations déréglées.' This final remark has led Gay and others to describe as the first edition of 1680 an edition of 420 pages and 36 obscene plates with an engraved title and imprint 'Venise chez Pierre Arretin [*sic*]' which clearly dates from *c.* 1775.

[7] The publishing history of the French original is curious. It originally appeared as *Lupanie, histoire amoureuse de ce temps*, 1668. Lupanie is the heroine who became Octavia in the English translation. In 1680 it appeared as *Saint-Germain, ou les amours de M.D.M.T.P.*, an attempt to link the story with Madame de Montespan. This was then reprinted as *Alosie*, possibly with a hint of Chorier's work. The original has been wrongly attributed to P. C. Blessebois; cf. F. Lachèvre's life of Blessebois (Paris 1927).

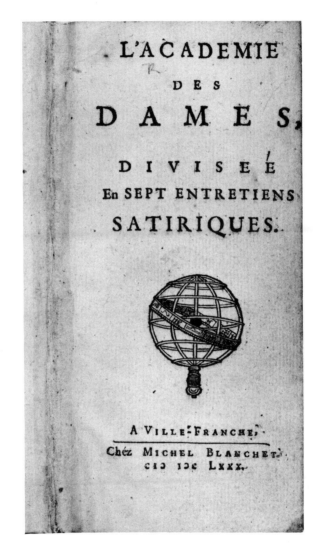

PLATE VIII. APPARENTLY THE ONLY SURVIVING COPY
The first edition of *L'Académie des Dames*, the first French translation of
Chorier's *Satyra sotadica*. 136×69 mm
(British Museum)

# A

# DIALOGUE

### BETWEEN

## A MARRIED LADY

### AND

# A MAID.

*LONDON:*

Printed in the Year M.DCC.XL.

PLATE IX. THE EARLIEST SURVIVING PROSE PORNOGRAPHY IN ENGLISH
An abridged English adaptation of Chorier's *Satyra sotadica*, first prosecuted in
1688. 152 × 86 mm
(Bayerische Staatsbibliothek, Munich)

ters have been changed to agree with Chorier's. The novel is itself a satirical attack on the wiles of an amorous bourgeois wife; it has some lively scenes, but is much closer to Boccaccio than to Chorier. Its appearance one year after the French translation of the *Satyra sotadica* shows at least that the English market knew about that translation and was eager to buy. But was there an English translation of the real thing at this time? The reference in Ravenscroft's *The London Cuckolds* of 1682 to 'the beastly, bawdy translated book called *the Schoole of Women*' must surely refer to *L'Académie des dames*.

In 1688 when Streater and Crayle were prosecuted we find 'a Dialogue between a Marridd Lady & a Maide' mentioned in Streater's bond, though it was not proceeded with at his trial. Hills's note of 'Tullia, Octavia, &c' identifies it more closely, and an edition of 1740 (collating A–D⁶) survives in the Bayerische Staatsbibliothek at Munich (Bibl. erot. Fr. Krenneri 840: Plate IX).[8] It is, of course, impossible to tell whether it is the same translation—or rather adaptation. The 1740 edition is particularly interesting because without softening the physical impact of the erotic scenes, and indeed using the Anglo-Saxon monosyllables as well as the elegant synonyms of the original, the whole is made much more innocent and closer to normal experience, so that it comes to have a similar tone to *L'École des filles*. It contains three dialogues, not the one the title suggests; the first follows the first dialogue of the original with slight abridgment, but the original second dialogue and most of the third which deal with Lesbian love-making are entirely omitted. The second dialogue of the adaptation, in which Tullia describes her wedding night to prepare Octavia for her impending marriage, is softened and made more natural throughout: the defloration is less sadistic, the encounters less frequent and Tullia more passive: this all comes from Chorier's fourth dialogue. Octavia's dream with Tullia's interpretation and her discourse in favour of a variety of sexual partners are omitted. The third dialogue, in which Octavia reports on what happened on her wedding night, is taken from the first quarter of Chorier's fifth book: the remainder, which reveals all the family skeletons,

---

[8] Graesse records a 12° of 46 pages as 'London, 1662(?)': the mark of interrogation is surely justified. Ashbee, *Catena*, p. 316n, notes that 'R. Borewell' in 1786 advertised a *Dialogue of a married lady and maid* which he had not seen.

condemned in more detail: 'Il faut que les plaisirs que nous pro-posons soient bornés par *les lois*, par *la nature* et par *la prudence*, et toutes les maximes dont ce livre pourroit t'instruire s'éloignent presque également de ces trois choses'.

Gay and the 'Geneva' [i.e. Brussels] reprint of 1868 speak of the first edition being undated and *c.* 1680 or 1682, but Lenglet du Fresnoy[11] in 1734 recorded as the first a 'Cologne' edition of 1683—all the early editions have a Cologne imprint. There are two candidates with this date, one with 166 pages (Wolfenbüttel, Dessau) and one with 204 (Berlin, Darmstadt, Weimar, etc.). These have three dialogues; the second, 'augmentée d'un entre-tien', is dated 1685 (pp. 214: Göttingen) and is followed by 1686 (*Gay*), a seventh edition of 1691 (pp. 204: Hamburg) and a possible variant of 1692 (pp. 204: Breslau). The BM has a 'sixth' edition of 1692 (pp. 107) which announces the fourth dialogue on its title-page but then has a note on the final leaf that the last dialogue has been dropped as it had been added by another hand. Not discouraged by this, another seventh edition 'augmentée d'un cinquième entretien' appeared in 1696 (pp. 205: Weimar) and an eighth in 1702 (pp. 216: BM, Dresden, Frankfurt, etc.). Graesse records another eighth edition of 1712; and yet another of 1719, which adds a fragment of a sixth dialogue, served as copy for the reprint of 1868. A 'Londres' edition of 1737 returns to the original three dialogues (BM, Halle).[12]

England was swift to produce a translation:[13] *Venus in the Cloyster, or the Nun in her smock* was advertised as published by Henry Rhodes in the *Term Catalogue* for Easter 1683. No copy has been traced of this or of the two editions translated by Robert Samber and published by Curll in 1724 and 1725 which caused the Court of King's Bench to define the law of obscene libel. A Curll catalogue of 1735 still advertises the work: was this just bravado? Finally a warrant of 8 April 1745 (PRO, SP.44/83/462) discloses 'that certain lewd and infamous books entitled "Venus in the

---

[11] *De l'usage des romans* vol. 2, p. 267.
[12] *La Religieuse en chemise, ou la nonne éclairée* (edition of 1763 in BM; reprinted 1860) is a different work on the same subject.
[13] Followed by the Germans in 1689 with *Die Venus im Kloster* (Berlin) and the Dutch in 1694 with *Venus in't Clooster* (H/G; also an edition of *c.* 1700: Darmstadt, Stuttgart).

Cloister or the Nun in her Smock in five Dialogues adorn'd with Curious Copper Plates" are now printing off by John Leake'; publication of this edition was evidently frustrated.

These then were the works which in original and translation held the field in England up to the series of prosecutions in 1745, where they were joined by the recently arrived *History of Don B* . (1743.) Here my story ends with the new dawn about to break on 22 November 1748 when the *General Advertiser* announced the first volume of John Cleland's *Memoirs of a Woman of Pleasure* (Fenton, 3s), followed by the second part in February 1749 (*Gentleman's Magazine*).[14] Here is the first original English prose pornography, and the first to break away from the dialogue form into the style of the novel. And whereas hitherto England relied on imports from Europe, she now became an exporter, and 'Fanny Hill' was translated and imitated all over the world.[15] There are, perhaps, few links between the old and the new, except those features pornography necessarily has in common. Most significant is that we still have a female narrator and that her name is Fanny, reminding us that the elder girl in *L'École des filles* was naturalized as Frances in the 17th century, and was called Fanny[16] in the edition of 1744. Perhaps Cleland's devotion to the elegant periphrasis introduced by John Armstrong in the *Œconomy of Love* is due to the prosecutions of 1745 where Anglo-Saxon monosyllables were much in evidence. But on a wider view the *Memoirs of a Woman of Pleasure* is important for its method rather than its content; the development of further excesses both in thought and action is left to the French.

## CONCLUSION

Since I have inevitably made certain judgments about the works I have discussed, and since judgments on this subject have

[14] Further details of the first publication of the *Memoirs* came to light after this article went to press, and they are to be found in the Appendix to this enquiry on p. 52.

[15] For the entertaining story of Isaiah Thomas and the first American edition, the sheets of which now bind the newspaper collection of the American Antiquarian Society, see Ralph Thompson's 'Deathless Lady' in *The Colophon*, new series vol. I, no. 2 (1935) pp. 207–20.

[16] Note also that Robinet became Roger, another example of the identification of characters with their *genitalia*.

little common basis, it seems reasonable that I should make some attempt to suggest a few principles which seem to me fundamental to the aesthetic and moral problems that pornography raises. Leaving aside for the moment society's attitude and what at any time is considered obscene, it seems that sex may be used in a work of art so that the reader may have a deeper understanding or a new view of life—whether the work is one of social realism, of satire, of fantasy, or of revolutionary thought. If a literary work can legitimately make us feel grief or fear, there seems no absolute aesthetic reason against it causing erotic excitement. At the other extreme are the books and pictures whose only purpose is to give form to erotic fantasies[17] for the gratification of the consumer, regardless of the realities of life and art; the cheap romantic novel, the sadistic thriller, and the pornographic book are all alike in releasing emotion by simple technical means which do not usually deepen the quality of our experience.[18] These have their function, and it may be a useful one: fantasy properly used, tested against reality, and left behind is an essential element of personal development; a temporary escape from the stresses and deprivations of real life may refresh; but the personality which clings to a fantasy view of the world is clearly sick. The fantasy of popular romance that wedding bells solve all problems has probably done more harm to modern society than the obscene, because it discourages the addict from facing the real problems that marriage entails.

There must inevitably be many border-line cases where it is impossible to agree on the category in which a book belongs; the serious writer may introduce a meretricious element into an otherwise good novel,[19] while a talented writer who produces a pornographic pot-boiler can scarcely avoid some valuable insights. It is the most important erotic works which raise the greatest difficulty of classification: the work of de Sade may serve as an example. The situation is complicated because once a book is

[17] I use the word 'fantasies' here in the popular sense, not as referring to entirely repressed unconscious material.

[18] A valuable analysis of the psychological tricks on which 'hard-core' pornography is based can be found in E. & P. Kronhausen, *Pornography and the Law* (New York, 1960).

[19] Cf. Walter Allen, 'The Writer and the Frontiers of Tolerance' in *To Deprave and Corrupt . . .'* (London, 1962) p. 151.

written the reader can use it as he wishes—children may find erotic desires stimulated by the Bible, while even commercial pornography may lead someone to a new perception of human problems. The prosecutions which have been listed here cut across any borderlines between pornography and literature that seem aesthetically justifiable.

When we turn to the problem as seen by society we are faced with the wide variation in attitudes to sexuality. A society like that of 5th-century Athens where the *Hermae* stood with erect phalluses outside every respectable house and were duly garlanded and anointed is in pointed contrast with our own which has had them removed from the public galleries of the National Museum in Athens. In any society, too, attitudes vary with class, and at a time when Martial's epigrams formed part of the classical education of an English gentleman a vernacular equivalent would have been regarded with horror. In modern Western civilization any form of sexual activity is so hedged with taboos that indulgence in it, even within the forms accepted by social conventions, has something of the quality of a revolt against authority. It is, indeed, difficult to escape the Freudian view of the Oedipal situation in which sexual activity is a direct challenge to the rights and authority of the father; and it is significant that all the books considered here and most of their successors are centred on the figure of the permissive female—the whore as against the father. Since sexual activity and writing of it is a revolt against authority, authority from time to time takes action against the revolt—or else authority is so repressive that revolt is the result. How the struggle progressed and what motives determined the attitudes of both sides at any given time can be given no satisfactory analysis; but it is clear that one passes from the period when Chaucer's most realistic tales were acceptable in mixed society and from the 16th century when Boccaccio's *Decameron* was expurgated of his attacks on the priesthood but not his erotic themes, to the 19th century when all sexual reference is suspect. On the side of literature, too, one can see that the writer becomes increasingly hostile to authority; by the 17th century the writing of sexual licence is linked with explicit attacks on religious and social conventions, and in the 18th century pornography has become obsessed with sexual orgies in religious or pseudo-religious orders, with the attack on the family in the theme of incest, and with the anarchism of de Sade. As in the family, so in society there must be some common cultural standards to enable a culture to survive; but since these are modified from generation to generation by the dynamics of the situation, I have tried not to take up a fixed position about society's role.

If then we turn from the books which society has found it necessary to attack to those which I would distinguish as hard-core pornography by the fact that their aim is principally to arouse sexual desire and encourage erotic fantasies, the remarkable fact emerges that the genre had a well-defined starting-point and a very rapid development.[20] We begin with *La Puttana Errante* about 1650 which turns the dialogue between whores from Aretino's satiric realism to an exposition of the means of sexual pleasure;[21] but it is still based on the brothel. *L'École des filles* in 1655 brings the subject into the private house, relating it to the realities of family life and also tying it to romantic love as against the conventions of society. By 1660 with Chorier's *Satyra sotadica* almost all the themes of later pornography are present; within a completely amoral attitude, in which all perversions are welcome if they gratify the senses, we have Lesbian love, sodomy, seduction of the young and innocent, multiple copulation, flagellation and more subtle forms of sadism. But above all, these take place within a tightly knit family circle, with the shocking suggestion that all the conventional relationships of society are merely a façade for personal gratification, into which even the local priest enters. This attempt to include the Church within the pattern is made explicit in *Vénus dans le Cloître* of 1683 and other contemporary works. Can this very sudden rise of a new form be explained?

Macaulay in his famous essay 'The Comic Dramatists of the Restoration' comments percipiently on the complete change of

[20] I am here speaking of prose writings. It seems to me that Giulio Romano's pictures and Aretino's sonnets are somewhat on the border line of pornography for all their obscenity: Aretino's claim that they are *jeux d'esprit* with classical precedents has some force. In any case the classification and psychological effects of verse and of pictures present problems different from those of prose and deserve separate treatment.

[21] It is noteworthy that Sinibaldus in 1642 and his followers still took the view that there was only one 'natural' posture and that this had a religious sanction; there was reason for a revolt.

tone and of morals both in the plots and in the attitude of the characters in the drama between say Fletcher and Wycherley; the change is certainly contemporaneous with the emergence of pornography and related to it—in, for example, the vanishing of the concept of sin. Macaulay goes on to explain the change as a natural and inevitable reaction against the enforced morality of the Puritans and as a product of the hypocrisy which that inevitably produced; but although there is surely truth in the idea of reaction after repression, we are not dealing purely with an English phenomenon—indeed, the pornography is all continental in origin. The repression must be seen in much broader terms—in the Reformation and the Counter-Reformation, which themselves follow earlier 15th-century attempts to do away with those 'abuses' which were safety-valves in an authoritarian society. Dale Underwood in *Etherege and the Seventeenth-Century Comedy of Manners* (New Haven, 1957) relates the change in the tone of the drama to the Europe-wide emergence of 'libertinism' as a fashionable and pervasive mode of thought whose freedom related to religion, politics, and society as well as to sexual life. Underwood traces many component strands, among which Epicureanism, Cynicism, and Pyrrhonism are prominent, and I cannot hope to summarize him here; but the chief feature he traces in English literature is the stress on the value of 'nature' and 'sense' as opposed to universal order or the laws of reason. In some ways this development runs parallel to Bacon's stress on the need for the direct observation of the senses rather than deference to the traditional authorities, or to the naturalism of Hobbes which sees the ruthless aggressive man beneath the forms of society. But these trends of thought are by no means only English: they run right across the European scene, though to my knowledge they have so far been studied only on a national scale.[22] It is clear that in some way the emergence of pornography is both stimulated and justified by these concepts, some of which continually recur in the texts; that society is based on hypocrisy and that the senses are to be preferred to authority are particularly prominent themes.

We must not lose sight of the relationship between libertinism

[22] e.g. René Pintard, *Le Libertinage érudit* (Paris, 1943) and G. Spini, *Ricerca dei libertini* (Rome, 1950).

and liberty. It is perhaps exceptional that in Britain liberty of the press is linked with the name of Wilkes who suffered equal fines and concurrent prison sentences for the seditious *North Briton* and the obscene *Essay on Woman*, but one cannot study the period without seeing how for both conformists and rebels one thing went with another.[23] When Mandeville's *Fable of the Bees* and Woolston's *Discourse on the miracles of our Saviour* were attacked by the grand juries of Middlesex in the 1720s, it was because they would lead to every sort of social discord and immorality, and most particularly to unnatural vice. From where we stand, the struggle for the right to free expression of religious and political ideas is a noble one and the cumbrous and denunciatory indictments somewhat comic; but to the 17th- and 18th-century conformists the idea of the free expression of heretical or revolutionary views must have been truly terrifying. The fear of sexual licence or immorality was socially a subsidiary one, though it might come more closely home to the individual to whom it was a more immediate threat. It seems that the revolt against authority first took the form of heresy, then politics, and finally sexual licence; clearly pornography is closely related to this revolt.

Though the works discussed here may originally have been written for a circle of libertine friends, the public for pornography was not to remain one of libertines. We come back again to Pepys and our first documented case of a man buying a dirty book—not his first, for he knew *La Puttana Errante* before he bought and burnt *L'École des filles*. For all his amorous adventures, one cannot describe Pepys as a libertine in any full sense of the word, and his criticisms of the practical libertinism of Court circles makes this explicit. It is, I think, more revealing to see Pepys in his role as the first great middle-class civil servant and to remember that it has probably been the apparently respectable (and often scholarly) professional man who has provided the bulk of the demand for pornography over the years. Supply and demand are related, and if the demand had existed a hundred years earlier, something would have appeared to meet it. Looking at Pepys and the 17th century one can see in historical develop-

---

[23] Mirabeau will serve as a French example of an important revolutionary figure who wrote much pornography.

ments possible clues to tensions which might explain the emergence of pornography.

Jung has pointed out the strain that the Reformation put on the individual Protestant; he could no longer rely on the authority of the Church, but had the duty to form his own beliefs on his reading of the Bible and to deal directly with God without the mediation of the priest—in many ways a terrifying burden. This idea of the individual's duty to decide spreads into politics and social life, a more responsible counterpart to the contemporary movements of libertinism, but still bringing with it further responsibilities and stress. In this same period, there seems to be the beginning of a parallel development within the family in the bringing up of children. Whereas children had formerly been thought of as owned by the family, 'apprenticed' from an early age to meet the family's needs, the child comes to be thought of and treated as a separately developing individual who matures and ideally enriches the family by mutual give and take; here again is the strain of individuation on the personality. Add to this the growth of the professional and middle-class virtues of economic individualism, clear thinking, orderly action, prudence, and responsibility, and primary emotions are under a heavy strain. All these forces begin to emerge in the 17th century, and they press most heavily on the responsible and intelligent. If, as some believe, pornography offers an escape from these pressures by regression to an infantile sexuality, its emergence in the 17th century is not inexplicable.

# JOHN CLELAND AND THE PUBLICATION OF THE *MEMOIRS OF A WOMAN OF PLEASURE*

I HAD NOT intended to deal with Cleland's notorious *Memoirs of a Woman of Pleasure* in my study of 'Libertine Literature in England, 1660–1745';[1] my dates were carefully chosen to exclude it. I had, however, discovered in the Public Record Office an important letter by Cleland on the subject, and just as the last part of my article was going to press a vital piece of bibliographical evidence turned up by chance after eight years' waiting. On looking at the published literature, including the new American edition,[2] it was clear that there was still a good deal of confusion that could be straightened out, and though I can give no final answer to all the problems which surround the publication of the book, at least some facts can be finally determined. I am greatly indebted to Mr John Hayward and Dr E. J. Dingwall for the use of their notes and observations.

The earliest advertisement I have found for the first volume is in the *General Advertiser* for Monday, 21 Nov. 1748:

> *This Day is Published, (Price 3s.)*
> MEMOIRS of a WOMAN of PLEASURE.
> Written by a PERSON of QUALITY.
> Printed for G. FENTON, in the Strand.

Subsequent advertisements drop the reference to the 'person of quality'.

The second volume is advertised in the *London Evening-Post* for 14–16 Feb. 1749:

> *This Day is publish'd, Price 3s.*
> *The Second and Last Volume of*
> MEMOIRS of a WOMAN of PLEASURE.
> Printed for G. Fenton, at No. 12, in Exeter Exchange in the Strand.

[1] *v.* THE BOOK COLLECTOR, Spring, Summer, Autumn 1963.
[2] G. P. Putnam's Sons, New York, 1963.

Later the imprint becomes 'Printed for G. Fenton, and sold at No. 12, in Exeter Exchange. . . . Where may be had, the first volume, price 3s.' Both volumes are advertised together at 6s in the *General Advertiser* of 27 March 1749.

After a considerable period of silence the government, apparently stirred by the bishops, went into action. On 8 Nov. 1749 a warrant[3] was issued by Newcastle to seize the author, printer, and publisher. The result is two informative documents, the first being Ralph Griffiths's statement[4] taken before Lovel Stanhope, the Law Clerk in the Secretary of State's office, on 13 November:

> Being shewn a Work in Two Volumes intitled "Memoirs of a Woman of Pleasure London printed for G. Fenton in the Strand 1749" & being asked whether he knows who is the Author, printer or publisher thereof, he says That some time last Winter his Brother Fenton Griffith came to him & asked his advice whether it would be safe for him to Publish the said Book; That at that Time there was only one of the said Volumes finished & the said Fenton Griffith giving the Examinant a discription of the said Volume the Examinant did advise him to publish it & the Examinant believes he did publish the same at his the said Fenton Griffiths Shop in Exeter Exchange in the Strand & supplied the Booksellers with it.
>
> The Examinant says that his Brother told him that he had the Copy of the said Work from one J. Cleeland who the Examinant believes, from what his Brother has told him, is the Author of the said Work.
>
> That the second Volume of the said Work was published by his said Brother about Seven Months since.
>
> The Examinant says that his said Brother has told him that Thomas Parker of Jewin Street in Aldersgate Street printed both the first & second Volume of the said Work.
>
> The Examinant says that he has sold about Sixty sets of the said Work now shewn to him.

This at last makes clear that the imprint 'for G. Fenton' is a simple cover for Fenton Griffiths, though one is entitled to wonder whether Ralph Griffiths was as detached an observer as he makes out. Fenton Griffiths does not seem to have been found by the authorities at the time.

Cleland wrote his own statement on the same day in the form of a letter to Stanhope;[5] it is a delightful piece of special pleading in all its varieties:

[3] *Copies taken from the records of the Court of King's Bench* (1763) p. 45.
[4] PRO, SP 36/111/159. I have expanded the contractions of the original.
[5] PRO, SP 36/111/157, 158.

Sir,

Called on to give an account of my Share in the Memoirs of a *Woman of Pleasure*; whatever may be the degree of guilt incurred by it, I shall at least deserve your favourable report by a most candid, and plenary detail of all the circumstances of it: Some indeed impertinent to a formal, judicial examination, but which may serve to abate much of the rigour urged against me.

The plan of the first Part was originally given me by a young gentleman of the greatest hopes that ever I knew, (Brother to a nobleman now Ambassadour at a Foreign Court,) above eighteen years ago, on an occasion immaterial to mention here.

This I never dreamt of preparing for the Press, till being under confinement in the Fleet, at my leisure hours, I altered, added to, transposed, and in short new-cast: when, on showing it to some whose opinion I unfortunately preferred to my own, and being made to consider it as a ressource, I published the first part. And not till near four months after the Second: which had been promised, and would most surely have never been proceeded to had I been in the least made sensible of the first having given any offence: and indeed I now wonder it could so long, escape the Vigilance of the Guardians of the Public Manners, since, nothing is truer, than that more Clergymen bought it, in proportion, than any other distinction of men.

And such at least was my tenderness of adding the fault of prophaneness, to that of wantonness, that in the second Volume, where the Story of the Flagellant is told, and which I fished for in actual life, I substituted a Lay-character, to that of a Divine of the Church of England, of whom the Fact, with little variation, is sacred Truth: as may, if doubted, on a slender enquiry be traced, and verified.

In short, my offence was really of itself a very severe punishment: condemned to seek relief, not only from the meanness of writing for a bookseller, but from becoming the author of a Book I disdain to defend, and wish, from my Soul, buried and forgot.

This too would probably be the Case, if the pious indignation of my Lords the Bishops will give them leave to consider that they can take no step towards punishing the Author that will not powerfully contribute to the notoriety of the Book, and spread what they cannot wish suppress more than I do. To say nothing of its giving occasion for this very natural question: why slept this zeal so long? and waked not but till the Book had had its run, and is dying of itself, unless they choose to give it new life?

May I support these arguments by an Example chosen from a Number? It is not eight months since the Son of a *Dean* and Grandson of a *Bishop* was mad and wicked enough to Publish a Pamphlet evidently in defence of *Sodomy*, advertised in all the papers.[6] This was perhaps rather overlooked

---

[6] There seems little doubt that the reference is to *Ancient and Modern Pederasty investigated and exemplified* which was listed among the books published in April 1749 by the *Gentleman's Magazine*. I have not traced a copy. Cleland's reference seems to have led to action: SP 44/134/9 contains a letter of 20 Jan. 1750 from Newcastle to the Attorney General sending the examinations of

than tolerated—What was the consequence? Why, it is at this instant so thoroughly forgot that few I believe know that ever such a Pamphlet existed: Whereas, if My Lords the Bishops had been so injudicious as to stir this stench they might have indeed provoked the public indignation, but its curiosity too: and all to punish a crazy wretch, who would, I dare swear, not be unambitious of taking Vanini[7] for his Model.

Thus far, sir, in mitigation rather than defence of my fault. I submit however gladly the whole to his Grace's decision. If the innocence of my intention, the circumstances in which I committed it, and even my present low abject condition, that of a writer for Bread, all are not sufficient to give, in his Grace's Eye, a less grave and serious turn to this affair, than a prosecution in form, in complaisance to this Episcopal Representation, which is however certainly of the latest; I must of course submit to superiour power. But it will be some alleviation to the rigour of my fate, if his Grace would permit me to be the *only* victim in this affair, and I do assure you, sir, if it proves of any service to the Reformation of manners, I shall not complain of being the victim; But it is really little more than Justice to acquitt, and deliver from longer confinement those poor People now under punishment for *my* fault: as they certainly were deceived by my avoiding those rank words in the work, which are all that they Judge of obscenity by, and made them think the Line was drawn between them, and all danger of Law whatever.

I scarce think it necessary to mention here, that, From the Messenger's house,[8] in the heat of my resentment at being treated like a common malefactor, I wrote a Letter to Mr Stone,[9] and probably a very impertinent one, but I take for granted that he must be too much the gentleman to use it against me: Especially since his not vouchsafing me any answer, was, from one of his extream politeness, mortification enough to a gentleman, who measuring other hearts by his own, would pay ten times more tender respect to the natural Jealousy of the distrest, than where, there is so little, and so vulgar a merit in paying it, to Fortune, and Power.

As for you, Sir, I shall not intrench on your time with anything so vain, and useless, as compliments from a Place like this, where my head is even so disordered that I can hardly write common sense, or common English. That Humanity you have showed me, is my security for your saying to yourself for me all that I ought to say, and with the more effect, in that I, from motives of diffidence, and respect, omit to say more.

I am, Sir, with the most profound sense of your goodness,

Your most obliged, and most

obed<sup>t</sup>, humble Servant

Dartmouth Street

Monday the 13<sup>th</sup>. Nov<sup>r</sup>. 1749.      J. Cleland

Thomas Cannon, the author, and John Purser, the printer, and requesting their prosecution. The further history of Cannon can be seen in a petition printed in *Notes and Queries* ser. 2, vol. 8 (1859), pp. 65–6.

[7] Lucilio Vanini, the Italian freethinker, burnt at the stake for atheism in 1619.

[8] The Messenger to the Press at this time was Samuel Grey, appointed in 1729.

[9] Andrew Stone, one of the Under-Secretaries of State.

On 24 November 1749, Stanhope wrote from the Secretary of State's office to John Sharpe of the Attorney-General's office[10] enclosing six recognizances in £100 taken before him for the appearance of the persons named at the Court of King's Bench on the last day of Michaelmas term. They were:

John Cleland of St. James's Place . . . Esq[r]
Thomas Parker of Jewin Street . . . Printer & Stationer
Ralph Griffiths of St Pauls Churchyard . . . Bookseller
Bispham Dickinson of London, Bookseller
Robert Sayer of Fleet Street London, Printseller
Matthias Darby of St. Martins in the Fields, Seal Engraver

The first three are, of course, author, printer, and publisher of the *Memoirs*. Whether the other three were involved in this or another case there is nothing to show.

It seems clear that the first three were not deeply intimidated, for in the *General Advertiser* of 8 March 1750 the following advertisement appears:

This Day is Publish'd,
*Compleat in One Pocket Volume, Price bound 3s.*
MEMOIRS of FANNY HILL.
*If I have painted Vice in its gayest Colours, if I have deck'd*
*it with Flowers, it has been solely in order to make the worthier,*
*the solemner Sacrifice of it to* VIRTUE.       Vide p. 273.
Printed for R. Griffiths, at the Dunciad in St. Paul's Church-yard.
*Of whom may be had, in Two Volumes, Price 6s.*
Memoirs of the celebrated Mrs. Lætitia Pilkington.

The entry in the catalogue of books in the *British Magazine* for March gives more information: 'Memoirs of Fanny Hill, (being the story of the heroine of a book published sometime since, entitled, Memoirs of a woman of pleasure, 2 vol.) divested of its obscenity . . .' This abridgment omitted all the details of the sexual encounters, but the Bishop of London, Thomas Sherlock, nevertheless wrote to the Secretary of State:[11]

Temple 15 March 1749.
My Lord Duke
   Your Grace ordered a prosecution against the Printer and publisher of the *Memoires of a Lady of Pleasure*. The same Bookseller, one *Griffiths* (as I apprehend) has published within a few Days a Book called *Memoires of Fanny Hill*, the Lewdest thing I ever saw; It is, I am told, the same with the other, after leaving out some things, which were thought most liable to

[10] SP 44/85/161.
[11] SP 36/112/139.

MEMOIRS

OF A

WOMAN

OF

PLEASURE.

VOL. I.

LONDON:
Printed for G. FENTON in the *Strand*,
M DCC XLIX.

PLATE x*b*. A later imitation. 158 × 97 mm
(Mr Graham Greene)

MEMOIRS

OF A

WOMAN

OF

PLEASURE.

VOL. I.

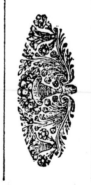

LONDON:
Printed for G. FENTON in the *Strand*
M.DCC.XLIX.

PLATE x*a*. The first edition. 156 × 95 mm
(British Museum)

*e*

*f*

*g*

PLATE XIII. More ornaments of Thomas Parker. Ornaments *f* and *g* are found in
the photographs of the lost *Memoirs of Fanny Hill* [1750]
  e. *Memoirs of a Woman of Pleasure*, 1749. (British Museum)
  f. *Travels . . . of William Bingfield*, 1753. (British Museum)
  g. *The Frisky Muse*, 1749. (British Museum)

the Law and to expose the Author and publisher to punishment—But if there is not Law enough in the Country to reach this vile Book after all the pretence to correct it, we are in a deplorable condition.

I beg of your Grace to give proper orders, to stop the progress of this vile Book, which is an open insult upon Religion and good manners, and a reproach to the Honour of the Government, and the Law of the Country.

I am My Lord
Your Grace's
most obedient & most humble servant
Tho: London.

On the same day, 15 March, a warrant was issued for the author, printer and publisher of *Fanny Hill*,[12] and on 20 March Griffiths made the following statement before Stanhope:[13]

> The Examinant says that upon the Suppression of a Book Intitled the Memoirs of a Woman of Pleasure he applied to Mr. Cleeland the Author of it, & desired him to strike out the offensive parts of it & compile a Novel from it which might be inoffensive, which the said Mr Cleeland did & called it "Memoirs of Fanny Hill" which the Examinant is the proprietor & publisher of.
>
> The Examinant says his motive for asking that Favour of Mr. Cleeland was that Mr. Cleeland owed him a Sum of money & as Cleeland was going abroad he thought it was the only Method to get his Debt paid.
>
> Says he does not think there is any harm in the said Book & that had the King's Messengers given him Notice that the said Book gave offence, he would have Cancelled the whole Edition.

At the same time a bookseller called William Owen made a statement that he had bought two copies from Jacob Robinson of Ludgate Street and 'lent one of them to an officer to read for sixpence'.[14]

Still Griffiths seems to have been unconcerned, for in his periodical *The Monthly Review* for March 1750 (published early in April) he reviewed *Fanny Hill* in the following terms:[15]

> Though this book is said to be taken from a very loose work, printed about two years ago, in two volumes, and on that account a strong prejudice has arisen against it, yet it does not appear to us that this performance, whatever the two volumes might be, (for we have not seen them) has any thing in it more offensive to decency, or delicacy of sentiment and expression, than our novels and books of entertainment in general have: For, in truth, they are

---

[12] *Copies taken from the records of . . . King's Bench*, p. 46.
[13] SP 36/112/145.
[14] SP 36/112/147.
[15] Vol. II, p. 431. Griffiths's authorship of the review is known from his file copy of the magazine in the Bodleian.

most of them (especially our comedies, and not a few of our tragedies) but too faulty in this respect. . . .

As to the step lately taken to suppress this book, we really are at a loss to account for it; yet, perhaps, all wonder on this head will cease, when we consider how liable great men are to be misinformed, how frequently obliged to see with other men's eyes, and hear with other people's ears.

★<sub>★</sub>★ The news-papers inform us, that the celebrated history of *Tom Jones* has been suppressed in *France*, as an immoral work.

On 12 April 1750, Newcastle, the Secretary of State, wrote to the Attorney-General a letter[16] reciting that Ralph Griffiths has been apprehended for printing and publishing ' "Memoirs of Fanny Hill", being an extract of a book entitled "Memoirs of a Woman of Pleasure", the author printer and publishers of which you have already had directions to prosecute'. He requested that Griffiths and Owen should be prosecuted on this new charge if there was sufficient ground. Nothing seems to have happened as a result of this request, and on 27 Nov. 1750 Newcastle wrote again, including the names of other printers and booksellers who were probably charged with other offences:[17]

The following persons, viz¹: Robert Sayer, John Cleland, Ralph Griffith, Thomas Parker, Charles Moseley, Henry Chappelle, Charles Corbett, William Owen, and George Bickham, being bound to appear upon their recognizances, in the Court of King's Bench, I am to signify you his majesty's pleasure, that you should prosecute them for the several crimes and offences of which they stand indicted . . .

Here, alas, the story fades into uncertainty. I have been unable to trace any action against these men up to the end of Hilary Term 1753.[18] There remains only the testimony of John Nichols, first in the *Gentleman's Magazine* (Feb. 1789, p. 180) and then in a slightly altered form in his *Literary Anecdotes* vol. 2 (1812) p. 458n. Having told of Cleland's being reduced to the debtor's prison, he goes on:

. . . In this situation, one of those booksellers who disgrace the profession, offered him a temporary relief for writing the work above alluded to,★ which brought a stigma on his name, which time has not obliterated, and which will be consigned to his memory whilst its poisonous contents are in circulation. For this publication he was called before the Privy Council; and the circumstances of his distress being known, as well as his being a man of some parts, John Earl Granville, the then president, nobly rescued him from the like

---

[16] SP 44/134/28; the copy is textually corrupt.

[17] SP 44/134/32.

[18] At this point there is over a year's gap in the 'Great Dogget Books'. A search of the Controlment Rolls and of the indictments has also been without result.

temptation by getting him a pension of 100l. a year, which he enjoyed to his death.

\* The sum given for the copy of this work was twenty guineas. The sum received for the sale could not be less than 10,000l.

The suggestion that Griffiths made £10,000 out of the *Memoirs* seems rather the fantasy of a jealous rival than a reasonable estimate; one wishes one could be sure of Nichols's other statements. Granville became Lord President of the Council on 17 June 1751, but there is no trace in the registers of the Privy Council up to the end of 1753 that Cleland ever appeared before them; indeed, it was not the sort of business they dealt with. It remains possible that Granville arranged a pension for Cleland— probably, no doubt, in the hope that he would lend his pen to the service of the government. One wonders whether Griffiths escaped legal action under a similar agreement—though the *Monthly Review* gained a good reputation for dispassionate criticism.

There remain the bibliographical problems. For a change, a number of copies of different editions survive or are reliably reported, and the problem is to determine which is the first edition. (It is always possible that the first edition has been lost; but since it enjoyed such a long period of immunity from legal action, it should be the most likely to survive.) We may, I think, safely discard the undated editions *Memoirs of* ★★★★★★★★★★ ★★ ★★★★★★★★★★★★, which Guillaume Apollinaire put first in his bibliography.[19] Since the first edition was advertised and referred to in the documents by its full name, the coyness of this title must be later—typographically it looks later as well.

This leaves us with four editions in which the title-page reads, with minor variations: MEMOIRS OF A WOMAN OF PLEASURE. VOL. I. [II.] *LONDON:* Printed for G. Fenton in the *Strand*, MDCCXLIX. G. Fenton, of course, is that shadowy character Fenton Griffiths; and the date 1749 in both volumes is natural enough even though the first was published in November 1748. The variations in the editions may be listed thus:

[19] In *L'Œuvre de John Cleland,* (Paris, 1910), p. 133, dating it 1747 or 1748. There are apparently two editions, one in the collection of Mr C. R. Dawes, pp. 232; 252 (A–I¹², K⁶, L²; A–K¹², L⁶) and two copies of the other in the Bibliothèque Nationale, pp. 228; 252. The untidy collation of Mr Dawes's copy suggests that it is the earlier; it has an MS inscription dated 1759.

A. Oval woodcut ornament on title-page. Date as 'M.DCC.XLIX.' 12°: A–I¹², K⁶; A–K¹², L⁶, M². Pp. [1–3] 4–227 [228 blank]; [1–3] 4–255 [256 blank]. 25 lines of type per page except vol. I, pp. 194–227 which are set unleaded, giving 29 lines. Headlines: *Memoirs of a | Woman of Pleasure*. With a sodomitical description in vol. II, pp. 177–9. BM, Yale, Bay Staatsbibliothek Munich, Bibliothèque Nationale. (Plate X*a*.)

B. A similar oval woodcut ornament on title. Date as 'MDCCXLIX.' 12°: A–I¹², K⁶; A–K¹², L⁶ (L6 not seen, presumably blank). Pp. [1–3] 4–228; [1–3] 4–250 [?251–2 blank]. 28 lines of type throughout. No headlines. Without the sodomitical passage. Mr Graham Greene. (Plate X*b*.)

C. Ornamental group of type-flowers on title. Date as 'MDCCXLIX.' 12°: A–I¹², K⁶; A–K¹², L⁶ as B, with which it corresponds page for page. No headlines. Without the sodomitical passage. BM, *Rothschild Catalogue* I, no. 643. (Plate XI*a*.)

D. No ornament on title. Date as 'M,DCC,XLIX.' Not seen; pagination reported by Apollinaire as 172; 187. Bay. Staatsbibliothek Munich (vol. I only).

Since it forms an important part of the argument, here is the description of the abridged version. No copy has been located, but there is a description and some photographs in a collection of notes put together by Michael Sadleir and now in the possession of Dr E. J. Dingwall.

MEMOIRS OF *FANNY HILL. If I have painted* Vice *in its gayest Colours, if I have deck'd it with Flowers, it has been solely in order to make the worthier, the solemner Sacrifice of it to* Virtue. *LONDON:* Printed for R. GRIFFITHS, in St. Paul's Church-Yard. [No date, but 1750.]
12°. *A*[3ll.] B–M¹², N[5ll.]; pp. [i–vi] [1] 2–273 [274 blank]. (Plate XI*b*.)

The work has been recast in the form of 11 letters (the last misnumbered 'xv'); it contains all the incidents of the original but not the sexual details, and as a result it is little over half as long. This text was reprinted as *Memoirs of the Life of the celebrated Miss Fanny Hill* . . . (London, printed by H. Smith, 1841: BM). No doubt copies are so rare because it was suppressed within a week of publication.

It is convenient to remove D from the list of four candidates for the first edition of the *Woman of Pleasure*; further argument will, I hope, confirm this step. The use of commas in the date 'M,DCC,XLIX' suggests a foreign origin, as does the fact that it is known by Apollinaire's description and a copy in Munich. The pagination is the same as a dated edition of 1781 described by Ashbee.

If we apply the same sort of general principles to A, B, and C, we can say that the changeover from woodcut headpieces and ornaments to the use of combinations of printers' flowers took place about 1750; some printers were quicker to take up the fashion than others. In general, though, the woodcut is typical of the first half of the century, and therefore A & B are likely to precede C. Similarly an irregular collation is more typical of a first edition than a regular one, since it is more difficult to estimate precisely the length of manuscript than of printed copy. On these grounds A would precede B & C: note not only the additional signature $M^2$ in vol. II but also the closer setting of type in sig. I of vol. I; these abnormalities are ironed out in the other editions.[20]

There is next the question of the sodomitical passage in vol. II. All editions record how Fanny's chariot had a breakdown on the way to Hampton-court, and how while waiting in an inn she observed a homosexual encounter in the next room. Only edition A includes two paragraphs which give the physical details in Cleland's usual periphrastic style. It has been widely accepted that these two paragraphs are a later addition, and they have been related to a note added by Bohn to his edition of Lowndes's *Bibliographer's Manual* (1864):

' . . . after this had appeared the language was considerably altered for the worse by Drybutter, the bookseller, who was punished for it by being put in the pillory in 1757'.

All attempts to find evidence to elucidate this statement have failed, but the suggestion that Drybutter added these two paragraphs scarcely fits the charge of altering the *language* for the worse. It seems to me highly improbable that Cleland, having deliberately led up to this scene, would not make the most of it as he did everywhere else. Moreover the references to sodomy in Cleland's letter trying to exculpate himself suggest that this point was being pressed against the book. If an indictment is ever discovered I would not be at all surprised to find this passage quoted in the charge. Subsequent publishers might then have a possible

---

[20] In the *Memoirs of* ********** ** ************ mentioned above it is interesting that one edition has an extra $L^2$ in the first volume; this suggests that A was used as copy and the compression of the text in $I^{12}$ was not noticed when the copy was cast off. This would therefore be the earlier of these two editions.

plea of innocence by claiming they had omitted the passage objected to. All this suggests to my mind that edition A which contains this passage is in fact the first edition.

The clinching evidence is that of the woodcut ornaments. Edition A uses three; the distinctive oval on the title-page (Plate XIIa); a rectangular cut of a common style with Cupid playing a lute (Plate XIIc) on the first page of text; and a double cornucopia of fruit and flowers (Plate XIIIe) at the end of vol. II. Of these, a is found on p. 48 and e on p. 26 of *The Frisky Muse* . . . *By Rigdum Funnidos* (London: printed for and sold by the author, 1749: BM); c appears on p. 1 of vol. 2 of *The Travels and Adventures of William Bingfield* (London: printed for E. Withers . . . and R. Baldwin . . . 1753: BM). These two books have other cuts in common to confirm that they came from the same printing shop.[21] Unfortunately there are no decisive breaks or signs of wear in the cuts which would establish the sequence in which these books were printed; but at least we have a rather naughty book of verse printed in 1749 by the same man who produced edition A.

Fortunately the photographs which are all that we have of the *Memoirs of Fanny Hill* show three ornaments. The one on the title-page (Plate XIIIg) appears on p. 42 of *The Frisky Muse*, and the one which heads the text (Plate XIIIf) is found in the same position in vol. 1 of *The Travels*. This too was therefore produced by the same printer. We know that the abridged *Memoirs of Fanny Hill* were printed for Griffiths in 1750; and when we find that the same printer was responsible for an edition of the *Memoirs of a Woman of Pleasure*, it is hard to escape the conclusion that this edition was the original one printed for Griffiths. In that case the printer was Thomas Parker, and like Griffiths and Cleland he was not deterred from making money out of *Fanny Hill* by the threat of court proceedings against the *Memoirs of a Woman of Pleasure*.

From this accumulation of evidence it seems clear that A is the first edition.[22] Edition B, which resembles it so closely, poses a

---

[21] The stock of ornaments is a mixed one, and looks as though it was acquired second-hand. There are certainly three cuts and probably more which belonged to Henry Woodfall in the 1730s; Woodfall senior died about 1747.

[22] It would not be surprising if there had been more than one edition printed for Griffiths in 1749, but all four known copies are certainly from the same setting of type in those pages of which I have had photostats.

problem. The key may be that it contains a frontispiece and eight hand-coloured mezzotints in each volume[23] which on expert evidence cannot be earlier than 1760. Most of them have volume and page references which fit edition B (and would approximately fit A and C as well). This suggests that we have a publisher planning an illustrated edition in the 1760s. The plates could be produced quite discreetly as required, but stock of a two-volume novel is not easy to conceal. It seems possible that the production of a reprint which could be explained away as a 'remainder' of the first edition might have its attractions—superficial attractions, no doubt, rather than any real preservative value against determined investigation; but this sort of publishing with its false dates and imprints is often satisfied with such rough cover. The woodcut ornaments on the titles and at the head of the text (Plate XII, *b* and *d*) are very similar to those in edition A, but they were probably already in existence and borrowed for this book: I have not traced their ownership.

Editions C and D, like the undated *Memoirs of* ★★★★★★★★★★ ★★ ★★★★★★★★★★★★, cannot at present be dated at all precisely; probably they never will be. Since it is in the highest degree improbable that Cleland ever revised the text, this is not of importance for textual study; if, as I hope I have shown, A is the first edition, we have the nearest we can get to Cleland's text, and it is not corrupt. But it would be nice to trace a copy of the original abridged *Memoirs of Fanny Hill.*

---

[23] The frontispiece to vol. 1 is probably a late insertion or replacement. The overall design of the plates is the same as some of the engravings attributed to Gravelot in an edition dated 1766 recently acquired by the BM: cf. *Cohen-de Ricci*, col. 243.

# INDEX